R. H. Tawney

LIVES of the LEFT is a new series of original biographies of leading figures in the European and North American socialist and labour movements. Short, lively and accessible, they will be welcomed by students of history and politics and by anyone interested in the development of the Left.   general editor   David Howell

published: **J. Ramsay MacDonald** Austen Morgan
James Maxton William Knox
Karl Kautsky Dick Geary
'Big Bill' Haywood Melvyn Dubofsky
A. J. Cook Paul Davies
R. H. Tawney Anthony Wright

forthcoming, to include: **Aneurin Bevan** Dai Smith
Thomas Johnston Graham Walker
Eugene Debs Gail Malmgreen
Ernest Bevin Peter Weiler

For Kettering Public Library,
a Tawney institution

LIVES
of the
LEFT

R. H. Tawney

Anthony Wright

Manchester University Press

Copyright © Anthony Wright 1987

Published by Manchester University Press, Oxford Road,
Manchester, M13 9PL, UK

British Library cataloguing in publication data
Wright, Anthony
    R. H. Tawney.—(Lives of the left).
    1. Tawney, R. H. 2. Socialists—Great Britain—Biography
    3. Historians—Great Britain—Biography
    I. Title   II. Series
    335.0092'4   HX244.7.T3

ISBN 0 7190 1998 2 *hardback*
ISBN 0 7190 1990 0 *paperback*

Set in Perpetua
by Koinonia Ltd, Manchester

Printed in Great Britain
by Robert Hartnoll (1985) Ltd, Bodmin, Cornwall

Contents

Preface

During a long and significant period, spanning much of the first half of the twentieth century, socialist thought in Britain was associated with the work of three domestic intellectuals. These were the Red Professors: G. D. H. Cole (1889-1960), Harold Laski (1893-1950) and R. H. Tawney (1880-1962). They were not a coherent group (indeed, they did not much care for each other), if they had important affinities there were also significant dissimilarities, but their collective influence was considerable. Taken together, their work illuminates much of the distinctive intellectual terrain of British socialism. Taken separately, as here, this terrain is approached from particular directions.

It is also approached from the vantage point of the present. What this reveals is that Laski's star, once the most politically brilliant of the three, has suffered a sharp decline into historical obscurity. The same fate seemed for a time to be in store for Cole, until a renewal of interest on the Left in non-statist socialist traditions gave his guild socialist ideas a strikingly contemporary significance. As far as Tawney is concerned, there was every reason in the decade after his death to expect, as did Margaret Cole, that 'his destiny is gradually to sink into comparative oblivion, along with some others in history whose personality bulked so much larger than their published work will indicate'.[1] As the memory of the man dimmed, so the interest in his work would also fade. Moreover, he had said what he had to say in the 1920s, in the trio of books (*The Acquisitive Society*, *Religion and the Rise of Capitalism* and *Equality*) which made his name, and went on saying very much the same things thereafter, which could make him seem an essentially historical figure who was unlikely to find a new audience. Yet this is precisely what has happened, as there will be occasion to record later, and Tawney has been turned to in the 1980s by those who have wanted to establish, or re-establish, the theoretical credentials of what is variously referred to as social democracy or democratic socialism. Whatever else this suggests, it at least suggests that there may be some timely merit in undertaking a fresh examination of Tawney's ideas.

That is what is attempted here. Because the focus is on the ideas, it is important also to recall the man. Beatrice Webb's verdict may stand for others: 'A scholar, a saint and a social reformer, R. H. Tawney is loved and respected by all who know him.'[2] He not only wrote about socialism, but seemed to personify it. Those who knew him were impressed, even overwhelmed, by his profound humility, but this did not prevent him (like other saints) from exhibiting a stubborn integrity and a prickly intolerance of cant. If he thought a principle was at stake, or a rule of conduct, then he could be very difficult indeed. Embroiled in a controversy about a proposed biography of Sidney Webb, Tawney refused to be mollified on the grounds that 'there are limits to my capacity to swallow humbug'.[3] Offered a peerage by Ramsay MacDonald, he replied with a terse inquiry about the harm he had ever done to the Labour Party. His rejection of materialism distinguished his personal life as much as his public work. Everyone thought him shabby, some thought him squalid. He was once described as the dirtiest man in the British Army. As Arnold Toynbee put it, Tawney 'could have shaken down easily among the Desert Fathers'.[4] If the personal side of Tawney is not explored here, this is not because it lacks interest or significance. His importance lies not just in what he did, but in how he did it.

If the man behind the ideas should be identified, then so too should the style in which those ideas were expressed. Michael Foot has remarked that 'Tawney's writings were read *and loved* – it is not too much to say – by one generation of Socialists after another',[5] but it is the *writings* which deserve emphasis too. He was a stylist, a writer of memorable English prose, with a powerful ironic punch. This was a gift, but it was a gift harnessed to sustained effort and application. Tawney's work, even quite minor pieces, usually went through several versions before it saw the light of day. When satisfied with a phrase or sentence, he was perfectly prepared to press it into frequent service. His irony could be elegant, but it could also be savage. If sometimes too elaborate and allusive quite to hit their target, his majestic, rolling sentences were usually steered with cumulating force and an instinctive sense of literary direction towards their crushing conclusion. Tawney knew what he wanted to say, and how he wanted to say it. His importance therefore lies not just in what he said, but in how he said it. The man, the style and the ideas are inseparable, even if it is the last of these which receives most attention in what follows.

In thinking about this book, and the larger tradition of which it forms a part, I owe a historic debt to my old friend Bob Rae, which I should like, at last, to acknowledge. In writing it, I have, again, been a preoccupied husband and father, and am grateful for being allowed to be (especially by Sam, who came with the book). My gratitude to Moira, my wife, includes this book, but includes everything else too. In the typing of it, all the credit belongs to Janet Francis, to whom I record my warmest thanks. The book is dedicated to a fine teacher, who introduced me to Tawney and much besides.

1 The education of a socialist

'My views, such as they are, have been formed by intercourse with working people'.

His name may have been Richard Henry Tawney, but no one ever called him that. To a handful of family intimates he was 'Harry', but to the rest of the world he was simply 'Tawney'. Having cast off much of his name, he dealt similarly with his origins. Born in India in 1880, where his father served church and empire as a notable Sanskrit scholar and principal of Presidency College in Calcutta, Tawney was to show no interest in his Indian background or the civilising mission. Nor did his larger and longer family history, studded as it was with bankers and brewers, interest him more. When the records of the Tawney banking house happened to find their way to the London School of Economics, and were even lodged temporarily in Tawney's own room, it nevertheless 'proved impossible to kindle in the great-grandson even a flicker of interest.'[1]

The family returned to England, to the comfortable England of Weybridge, when Tawney was still very young and he underwent the conventional education of his age, class and sex. First, for this future scourge of the public schools, there was Rugby, for a sound classical education (and for the beginning of a long and important friendship with William Temple, the future Archbishop of Canterbury). Then, for this future reformer of the ancient universities, there was Balliol College, Oxford, a far more decisive experience. It is difficult at this range to get inside the atmosphere of turn-of-the-century Balliol, with its particular

mixture of scholarship and social concern, but it clearly contained
elements capable of producing a powerful and durable response
in many of those who breathed it in. The influence of T. H.
Green was still strongly felt, with its Idealist analysis of the
derivation of rights from functions and its consequences for a
'politics of conscience'.[2] There was also the emphasis on social
service, a doctrine of social duties and responsibilities, which
could take many forms but which was an explicit part of the
Balliol ethos during the years of Edward Caird and A. L. Smith.
It is reflected in the recollection by William Beveridge, Tawney's
friend, contemporary and (after 1909) brother-in-law, that they
both left Oxford inspired by the severe injunction of Caird, the
Master of Balliol, that 'when we had done with Oxford studies,
some of us should go to Poplar to discover why with so much
wealth, there was also so much poverty in London'.[3]

In embarking upon this search, Tawney carried other influences with him. As a Christian (the fact is simply stated, but this
should not obscure its overwhelming centrality), Tawney was
interested in ideas which explored the social significance of Christian doctrines. In this he was greatly influenced by the social
gospel of Charles Gore, later Bishop of Birmingham (and to
whom Tawney was to dedicate *Religion and the Rise of Capitalism*).
Over the Balliol wall, in St John's College, there was Sidney Ball,
the leading figure in Oxford socialism at the time who, in Tawney's first term, had published a celebrated article on 'The
Socialist Ideal' which argued the case for an ethical socialism in
terms which Tawney was later to make his own. Then, further
removed but no less personally felt, was the influence of Arnold,
Ruskin and Morris, nineteenth-century voices but with clear
echoes in the indictment drawn up against twentieth-century
'civilisation' (to use Morris's pejorative term) by Tawney as he
began to examine and experience English society in the first years
of the century.

It is, perhaps, possible to make too much of such assorted 'influences'. As Tawney himself once remarked, 'historians of political thought are apt to be obsessed with origins and pedigrees, as though ideas were transmitted in the same manner as property'[4] (adding – his subject was the Webbs – that 'original people are not links in a chain, more often they are breaks in one'). Yet breaks require tensions and pressures, of both a positive and negative kind, affecting the nature and direction of the break when it occurs. In Tawney's case, some of these were already in evidence by the time he went down from Oxford in 1903, although the most important were still to come. An awkward examinee, handicapped by slow writing and an insufficiently narrowed mind, Tawney took a Second in 'Greats' (prompting Caird to comment on the examiners' failure to detect 'the chaos of a great mind' but also his father to ask how he 'proposed to wipe out this disgrace').[5] Speaking to LSE students in the 1950s, their emeritus professor happily confessed that 'having preferred the decorous obscurity of an un-ostentatious second to the meretricious brilliance of a spectacular first I have some hesitation about the problems connected with a student's academic life. . .'[6]

It was after Oxford that Tawney's most formative education began, as he always enjoyed pointing out (usually in a phrase about the process of 'getting over' his education). His first passage, in the company of Beveridge, was from Balliol to Toynbee Hall, the university settlement in the East End of London then presided over by Canon Samuel Barnett. It was a passage from social concern to educational social work, conventional enough in its own terms, but an important staging post for Tawney and many others. It involved Tawney in both social investigation and teaching and 'from the start he developed a strong sense of the East End'.[7] However, he also had to find a job and, after considering and rejecting the Charity Organisation Society, accepted the post of secretary to the Children's Country Holiday Fund. He held the post for three years, until 1906, combining it with his voluntary work at Toynbee Hall. As well as running a range of courses there, increasingly on economic and political topics, he investigated and campaigned on trades boards, juvenile labour, unemployment relief and university reform. On the latter, Beveridge reported to his father than an 'outraged' Oxford was 'blaspheming, horribly' after the appearance of one Tawney article.[8]

It is clear, then, that Toynbee Hall was important for Tawney in a number of ways. There was the direct contact with poverty and social distress, but also the experience of the solidarity and 'humanity' (Tawney's word at the time) of working-class life in the East End. There was the direct observation of the decline of religious observance, the fact that 'one of the great social forces of history is gradually and reluctantly drifting out of the lives of no inconsiderable part of society', but also the attribution of this to the squalid conditions occasioned by an equally squalid 'ethical atmosphere'.[9] Tawney was to have more to say about that before long. There was, too, an increased sense of the inadequacy of a charitable and philanthropic approach to social distress and of the need to tackle its structural causes. If this took Tawney beyond the prevailing parameters of the Charity Organisation Society, it also made him sensitive to the limitations of Toynbee Hall and the Canon Barnett approach to these matters. He did not renounce Toynbee Hall (in fact, he lived there for two further periods before 1914) but had come to feel that 'a locality is not satisfied by a club of the cultural'.[10] It was something, but not enough, either for a locality or for Tawney.

He had decided that he wanted to teach. More precisely, as he wrote to Beveridge, 'teaching economics in an industrial town is just what I want ultimately to do'.[11] He wanted a particular subject, with a particular audience, for a particular purpose. A personal preference had already fused with a strategy for social change. However, this was not to be his immediate destination. In 1906 he went to Glasgow University, as an assistant in economics, an experience which both produced his friendship with Tom Jones (who was later to be the mandarin adviser to several prime ministers, and the reason why Tawney phrases were even to find their way into Stanley Baldwin's speeches) and cured him of any desire to be an economic theorist. He was later to recall how he 'exchanged apples for nuts in the best manner of Marshall' and 'discoursed on marginal utility with the gravity appropriate to the recondite truth that, when one has eaten one breakfast, one is not equally eager for another'.[12] While in Glasgow he also wrote radical leaders for the *Glasgow Herald* (until the paper 'found me out'), the start of a long subsidiary career as a leader writer and generally anonymous commentator on educational issues in the serious press, mainly in the *Manchester Guardian*.

Tawney could have left the Glasgow job for journalism. In the event, he left it (in 1908) for the job which not only enabled him to do what he had long hoped to do, but which was also to form a vital, decisive part of his own political education. The Workers' Educational Association had been founded in 1903, with Albert Mansbridge as its pioneering spirit, to provide liberal adult education to working people. Tawney had joined its executive in 1905, and soon afterwards brought in William Temple as the WEA's first president. For Tawney this was the beginning of nearly half a century of identification and involvement with the WEA, for a large slice of that time (1928-1945) as its tireless president.

The first task, though, was to forge an alliance with the universities in the cause of extension education. This was the purpose of the Oxford conference which issued in the celebrated 1908 report on *Oxford and Working Class Education,* and in which Tawney's hand, though not his signature, was clearly visible. In response to local demand, tutorial classes had already been established at

R. H. Tawney

Longton (in the Potteries) and at Rochdale, with Tawney selected by Mansbridge as their tutor; but as a result of the Oxford conference these classes were now sponsored by the Oxford University Tutorial Classes Committee, which became Tawney's employer. The classes have become a legend in the history of English adult education.[13] They were undoubtedly important for Tawney, in their purposive fellowship, in their sense of a class preparing itself for power, and in their fusion of education and social commitment. Tawney now felt *useful,* in a role which combined teaching and scholarship with the cultivation of the soil upon which durable social change could be constructed. 'If I were asked', he once said late in life, 'where I received the best part of my own education, I should reply, not at school or college, but in the days when as a young, inexperienced and conceited teacher of Tutorial Classes, I underwent, week by week, a series of friendly, but effective deflations at the hands of the students composing them'.[14]

If Tawney took much from these classes, he also put a lot in. It was a gruelling routine, as he set out each week from Glasgow to travel between his four classes (in Rochdale, Longton, Littleborough and Wrexham), a routine eased at least somewhat when he set up home in Manchester after his marriage to Jeanette Beveridge in 1909. Moreover, the Tutorial Classes Committee had further decided (in a move sufficient to chill the blood of a modern extramural tutor) that, in lieu of a fifth class, Tawney should 'prepare a book on the Industrial History of the late 15th and early 16th centuries'.[15] The students wanted a historical approach to economic problems and Tawney supplied it. He had become an economic historian, for their need was also his own. As he was to put it in his Inaugral Lecture at the LSE, he 'found the world surprising' and 'turned to history to interpret it'.[16]

The records of Tawney's tutorial classes testify to the diligence of his preparation, his determination to keep up the standards of the classes, his attention to the needs of individual students (several of whom, like A. P. Wadsworth – the youngest member of the Rochdale class and future editor of the *Manchester Guardian* – were to achieve distinction), and the general good fellowship. They also reveal that Tawney was already an economic historian of a distinctive kind, careless of academic demarcation lines and approaching the subject in a spirit of moral inquiry. On the first essay from E. S. Cartwright, the Longton class secretary, Tawney wrote: 'Our problem at the present day is to put economic activity in proper relation to the other elements of life. But if we forget the economic motive altogether and overlook the material conditions on which the production of wealth depends, we become mere sentimentalists and dreamers'.[17] This comment captured the essence of Tawney's own agenda, at once both academic and political, material and moral. Moreover, in his classes he was already seen as a political figure, who called himself a socialist (he had joined the Fabian Society in 1906, and the Independent Labour Party in 1909). Reporting on the 1909-10 session, the Rochdale class secretary wanted to point out that their tutor had 'established for himself a position in the town, especially among Labour men, and his withdrawal from Rochdale would be looked upon as a calamity by a far larger circle than the members of the Class'.[18]

Tawney spent five happy and formative years in Manchester. He was practising a philosophy of education as the route to self-development, than which there was no higher human purpose, but also as the route to a remoralised social order. He was teaching and researching in a subject which taught the lesson that the present economic basis of society was simply one episode in a longer story of historical experiences and possibilities. He was making important friendships, especially with the economic historian George Unwin, who exercised a considerable influence (despite their political differences) on Tawney's approach to economic history.[19] He was also, because immediate problems mattered too, continuing to examine the exploitation of juvenile labour, made visits to Germany to examine their social policy machinery at first hand, and gave evidence to the Poor Law Commission in which he commended the German example of regarding unemployment as an industrial disease not as a failing of individual character. In 1912, Tawney was appointed director of a foundation, the Ratan Tata Foundation, which had been established under the wing of the London School of Economics with an endowment from an Indian business magnate to 'promote the study and further the knowledge of methods of preventing and relieving poverty and destitution'. The additional demands which this imposed inevitably curtailed the number of his classes and eventually, with 1914 approaching, brought him back to London.

By 1914, then, Tawney's education as a socialist was virtually complete. Moreover, it was already bearing fruit, of different kinds, but all with a distinctive quality which indicated their common source. This can be seen by looking briefly at some of the matters upon which he had spoken and written by this time. There was his economic history, above all his study of *The Agrarian Problem in the Sixteenth Century* (1912), dedicated to Temple and Mansbridge of the WEA, and recording its author's debt as 'a fellow worker' to the tutorial classes where 'the friendly smitings of weavers, potters, miners, and engineers, have taught me much about problems of political and economic science which cannot easily be learned from books'. The commission to Tawney to produce a book that would be useful in the classes had in fact produced a masterpiece, a triumphant combination of scrupulous scholarship and moral commitment. It stands in a distinguished line of historical writing which includes the Hammonds' *The Town Labourer* and, further away in time but nearer in provenance, Edward Thompson's *The Making of the English Working Class*. 'If in any degree the book can be called the outcome of the Workers' Educational Association', wrote the leading economic historian, W. J. Ashley, in review, 'then for the scholar, at any rate, the WEA is beginning to be justified by its fruits'.[20]

In mapping the agricultural changes produced by the effect of large-scale enclosure on customary rights, Tawney emphasised that here was not simply a chronicle of economic change nor even of the changing basis of economic power, but also the arena for contending conceptions of the proper conduct of economic and social life. 'Economic policies are not to be explained in terms of economics alone', he insisted; for when 'an old and strong society is challenged by a new phenomenon, its response is torn from a living body of assumptions as to the right conduct of human affairs, which feels that more than material interests are menaced, and which braces itself anxiously against the shock'.[21] The historical investigation of 'assumptions as to the right conduct of human affairs', especially in their economic aspects, was the field which Tawney was to make his own.

However, it was also already clear that this was to be a historical investigation with a resolutely contemporary purpose. As director of the Ratan Tata Foundation, Tawney published monographs on the operation of the minimum rate provisions of the 1909 Trade Boards Act in the chain-making and tailoring industries, demonstrating the beneficial effects of these provisions. At the same time, though, as economic historian, he undertook a study of Elizabethan wage regulation under the Statute of Artificers of 1563, 'a piece of regulation as characteristic of the economic environment of the sixteenth and seventeenth centuries as, in a widely different sphere, factory legislation is of modern industry'.[22] This was the answer to those who denounced the revolutionary character of legislative interference with economic relationships, since such interference was, in historical terms, the rule and not the exception. It was also the beginning of Tawney's long and

sustained mission to demonstrate to his fellow countrymen that
the brief interlude of unregulated capitalism should be seen as
just that, as an economic and moral aberration when viewed
against the whole course of human history, and not accepted as
an eternal verity.

In surveying some of the main elements of the position that
Tawney had arrived at by 1914, there are a number of further
revealing landmarks. One of these is his inaugural lecture, in
1913, as director of the Ratan Tata Foundation, where he
described the 'spirit' in which he would be approaching the
research into poverty. There would be no 'superstitious reverence
for accumulated facts', in the manner of so much current social
research, since he did not believe 'that the future welfare of
mankind depended principally upon the multiplication of
sociologists'.[23] If some problems undoubtedly required more
knowledge before they could be addressed, there were more
areas where 'the continuance of social evils is not due to the fact
that we do not know what is right, but to the fact that we prefer
to continue doing what is wrong' for, added Tawney in a characteristic aphorism, 'those who have the power to remove them
have not the will, and those who have the will have not, as yet,
the power'. Moreover, the focus of research into poverty should
be on causes not symptoms, structures not individuals, remedies
not palliatives, the normal not the abnormal. The real problem
was 'the economic status and opportunities of those who make
up seven eighths of the community, not of a submerged
residuum'. This meant, in the words of his title, that poverty
was above all an industrial problem, to be studied 'in the mill,
in the mine or at the docks, not in casual wards or on the
Embankment', and that the right approach was, through various
forms of public intervention, to strengthen the 'economic resist-
ing power' of the mass of the population. This would in turn,
Tawney believed, encourage both independence and mutuality,

instead of a degrading and resented dependence upon either charity or bureaucracy. Finally, Tawney rounded on those character-improvers in the poverty industry ('improve the character of individuals by all means – if you feel competent to do so, especially of those whose excessive incomes expose them to peculiar temptations') and attacked the 'hypocrisy of suggesting that it is possible to combine the moral advantage of a certain type of character with the economic advantage of industrial arrangements in which that type is shown by experience to deteriorate'.

Tawney did not, of course, disparage the concern with 'character'. Indeed, it was to be one of his central themes, as he hammered away at the connecting thread between character, condition and system. He reserved his sharpest arrows for those who, despite protesting their concern with character and moral improvement, refused to make this connection. This argument was deployed, and extended, in Tawney's celebrated 1914 essay 'An Experiment in Democratic Education', a powerful expression of the ideological underpinnings of his approach to adult education.[24] What the adult education movement had done was to challenge the prevailing assumption that education and character could properly be divided by class. This 'differentiation of humane education according to class' was an affront to those on whom it was practised and a degradation in those who practised it. The latter, not least to be found in the universities, who needed to be taught what education, culture and character were really about, were directed by Tawney to the WEA, where men were 'building from within', and to the tutorial classes where 'to these miners and weavers and engineers who pursue knowledge with the passion born of difficulties, knowledge can never be a means, but only an end; for what have they to gain from it save knowledge itself?' In other words, the challenge from the adult education movement was to the *whole* philosophy and organisation of education in England – 'the beautiful English arrangement by which wealth protects learning and learning in turn admits wealth as a kind of honorary member of its placid groves' – and, because the educational system reflects the values of the wider society, to the social system too. Tawney was to return to this theme, of education as the exemplar of social values, on many future occasions.

There is enough, then, in Tawney's published work by 1914, to indicate many of the leading elements in his social thought. His work in economic history, on social problems, on education, was clearly not to be seen as a series of separate enterprises but as a unified project, reflecting a common approach and rooted in a common stock of ideas and values. It was not until after the Great War that this project was to be given systematic expression, in the famous series of books which established his reputation. However, there is another book, never intended for publication and eventually published only many years after his death, which fortunately enables us to get much closer to the Tawney of 1914 and to understand some of his most fundamental beliefs, values and ideas. This is the diary, or commonplace book, which Tawney kept in that crucial period between 1912 and 1914 while he was living in Manchester. It simply bore the legend: 'If found, please return to R. H. Tawney, 24 Shakespeare Street, C-on-M, Manchester. PRIVATE'. Not merely is it a fascinating, indeed unique, historical document of the period, it is also an indispensable document for an understanding of Tawney. The WEA journal reported at this time that 'Birkenhead, Birmingham and Swindon, Belfast, London and Longton, are at the moment grappling with R. H. Tawney upon the need for a unifying centre for ethical precept'.[25] How Tawney himself was grappling with this matter is written across the pages of his commonplace book.

It is a sustained private meditation on the contemporary human condition, undertaken by someone who felt this condition in a direct, intense and personal way, but who was not the sort of person to disclose so much of himself in public, either in his writings or in correspondence, even when dealing with these same great issues. In his published work they are presented as issues for society; but here they are issues for Tawney. As he chews over comments made to him (frequently by members of his classes), or mulls over reported remarks and published articles, he tosses out his own questions and suggestions, along with a note about how these may be taken further. This may involve an attention to the significance of a particular historical event (reflected, for example, as the lecture notes for his tutorial classes reveal, in his courses at this time on the French and American revolutions); or the need to pursue a potentially fruitful line of historical research (with at least one such line – 'I wonder if Puritanism produced any special attitude toward economic matters'[26] – destined to yield a famous harvest of fruit under Tawney's later cultivation); or the insights to be gained by assembling historical materials around a particular theme (as with his outline of a book, one of many he wants to write on assorted topics 'if ever I have the chance', on 'Economic Privilege and Economic Liberty'). Above all, though, Tawney's main task is to accommodate this range of contemporary opinion, current events and historical reflection within the framework of a unified approach, which could not only make sense of the society around him but also indicate a way in which that society could find a durable solution to the industrial and social problems increasingly tearing it apart.

What, then, for Tawney was the basis for such a unified, and unifying, approach? In essence, it involved a recognition that these problems were at bottom moral ones. The point is made in different contexts, with different issues in focus, but it is always Tawney's essential theme. Once he has it between his teeth, like his adored dog, he bites on it furiously and refuses to let it go. 'The industrial problem is a moral problem', he writes, 'a problem of learning as a community to reprobate certain courses of conduct and to approve others'. It should be possible for a community, especially one with a common moral and cultural tradition, to achieve a basic agreement on the proper rules of conduct of social and economic life. Indeed, while it is necessary and desirable that there should be political disagreement about means, the same is not true about ends. There should not be 'variety in standards as to fundamental questions of conduct', for this 'does not only divide parties, but poisons social life'. It is the absence of such agreed standards which is the real source of social strife. 'It ought to be possible', mused Tawney in 1913, 'to place certain principles of social and economic conduct outside the sphere of party politics, as agreed upon by the conscience of the nation. . . Could not one find some formula expressing the attitude of all good men to social questions, which should be so entrenched in public conviction as to be drawn into dispute by no party?'

If it was asked where such a formula was to be found, or how it was to be discovered, Tawney had no difficulty in supplying an answer. It required no elaborate exercises in moral or social philosophy, merely a drawing from the well of moral knowledge which is 'the common property of Christian nations'. The existence of such common moral property was evidenced by the fact that its propositions won assent when stated in general terms, but the task now was to operationalise them in the conduct of social and economic affairs. Once this was accepted, then research into social problems would cease to be disconnected and diffuse, but would instead acquire a clear purpose and focus. Like the jurist who develops the law by bringing new cases within the framework supplied by general legal principles, the sociologist 'ought to build up his science by bringing new economic cases under some of the rules of conduct generally accepted by civilised men'.

It will be necessary, in later chapters, to discuss Tawney's views on this and other matters, but for the moment it is enough to register the fact that these are the views he holds. He does believe, without apology or embarrassment, that it is quite possible to distinguish 'right' from 'wrong', in economic affairs no less than in private conduct; that the failure to act upon this distinction is the source of the contemporary social and industrial unrest; and that moral reconstruction is therefore the prerequisite for economic reconstruction and social peace. These are the perspectives which inform everything he thought and wrote at this time, and which were to shape the rest of his life's work.

His analysis of contemporary events clearly reflects this general position. Writing at the height of the pre-1914 'labour unrest', Tawney interprets this industrial turbulence not as a materialist struggle about wages and rewards but as a demand for a new moral order in industry. It is to be seen as a protest against an economic system which is felt to be morally out of joint, and as a refusal by workers to be treated merely as hands or tools, as means not as ends. Thus 'the indictment brought by workers against modern industry is in essence that brought in all times against slavery: viz that under present arrangements men are used not as ends but as means'. Tawney frequently compares the struggle against slavery, a struggle which he describes as a story of moral growth and eventual victory, with the modern struggle against industrial autocracy. Similarly, he cites the achievement in the modern world of religious and political liberty as part of a process of moral advance which now required to be extended by the addition of economic liberty. This was the real significance of the labour unrest. 'This has been a wonderful year', wrote Tawney in 1912, adding: 'I think the cause of the unrest is mainly that the street corner preaching is at length beginning to have effect'.

It is upon the basis of this kind of moral analysis that Tawney assesses not merely current events and problems but also the approaches applied to these matters by assorted groups of social reformers. Tawney believes that most of these approaches are deeply flawed, both in their analysis and their proposed remedies. Thus 'one whole wing of social reformers has gone. . . altogether astray' in believing that the social problem is about the relief of distress: 'The supreme evil of modern industrial society is not poverty. It is the absence of liberty, i.e. of the opportunity for self-direction; and for controlling the material conditions of a man's life'. In an interesting passage Tawney describes the 'stages of thought about social affairs' through which he (and perhaps others) have passed. First, there was the belief that social problems are to be seen in terms of individual misfortunes or failings (the Charity Organisation Society stage); then replaced by the belief that they have to be viewed as structured by a social system, requiring action by the state to effect alterations to this system (the theoretical socialist stage); but in turn displaced by a third stage when 'one realises that the attitude of the state is just the attitude of countless individuals'. Once this is realised, then although the approach of the state to social questions remains 'profoundly wrong', it is seen to be wrong 'because the attitude of individuals to each other is wrong, because we in our present society are living on certain false and universal assumptions'. It is, therefore, not a subsidiary or unnecessary task but the *first* task to effect a change in these assumptions and principles.

The failure to understand this is where the Fabians are 'inclined to go wrong', just as the Marxists are 'not revolutionary enough'. For similar reasons, although it is important that economies should be so organised as to yield increasing wealth, it is an error to believe that increased wealth by itself is the path to a more contented society. Such a belief is falsified by the whole course of modern economic history, when the 'growth of moral dissatisfaction has synchronised with an unprecedented growth in material resources'. The conclusion to be drawn from this is clear:

> It is that what one may call a 'satisfying social system' is very largely independent of the material environment. The latter will not by itself bring the former, because the two things are not in *pari materia.* You cannot achieve a good society *merely* by adding one to one till you reach your millions. The social problem is a problem not of *quantities,* but of *proportions,* not of the *amount* of wealth, but of the *moral justice* of your social system.

When the labour movement gives expression to this it stands, as it essentially does, for freedom; but it has made the 'one tragic mistake' of pursuing comfort instead of rights. That path will eventually turn out to be a cul-de-sac, for when riches are redistributed 'will not the world, with its present philosophy, do anything but gobble them up and look with an impatient grunt for more?' That, says Tawney, is 'the real question', and adds that:

> It will not be faced in my lifetime because as long as the working classes believe, and believe rightly, that their mentors rob them, so long will they look on the restoration of the booty as *the* great reform, and will impatiently waive aside more fundamental issues. . . But when their masters are off their backs they will still have to face the fact that you must choose between less and more wealth and less and more civilisation.

In reading these striking passages from Tawney's pre-1914 diary, there can be no doubt about the sort of mind we are meeting. Perhaps three characteristics in particular stand out. It is the mind of a historian, a moralist, and a Christian. The historian's mind constantly reaches out to set the contemporary situation within a historical frame of reference, separating the current from the eternal, the particular from the universal. In looking back at the historical process out of which the modern world emerged, in being a reformer who does not expect the decisive reformation to occur during his lifetime, in looking forward to the time when 'three or four hundred years hence mankind looks back on the absurd preoccupations of our age with economic issues with the same wonder as, and juster contempt than, we look back on the theological discussions of the middle ages', in all these aspects Tawney's mind reflects a profound historical sense. It is a mind which is unlikely to confuse the fashion of the moment, whether intellectual or economic, with the historical destiny of humankind, or to allow such confusion and mystification to go unchallenged when practiced by others.

It is also, and conspicuously, the mind of a moralist. It exhibits a resolute belief in the primacy of moral ideas in social action and of the moral terrain as the real arena of battle. Institutions and mechanisms are always 'fed from without', by a prevailing social philosophy:

> All that a statute can do is to reduce a philosophy (important or trivial) into sections which are sufficiently clear to be understood even by lawyers. Hence the great days of a Parliament are when there is outside Parliament and in society a general body of ideas which Parliament can apply. It has no *creative force*. There *is* no creative force outside the ideas which control men in their ordinary actions. There is no *deus ex machina* who can be invoked though men are always trying to discover one. Nor is the modern futility of Parliament due to mechanical difficulties, which can be removed by mechanical remedies, such as revolution. It is due to the absence of any general accepted philosophy of life. Our principal task is to create one.

Thus the first task was to clear the ground of false standards and principles and construct in their place a true social philosophy, then to proceed to 'objectify our morality' in social institutions. This, of course, was precisely the dual task which Tawney was to set himself.

Finally, but not last in importance, it is the mind of a Christian.

Tawney wrote and spoke little about the deepest sources of his beliefs and was profoundly uninterested in matters theological. Although he was always lecturing the church on its social duties, and moved in high Anglican circles, his writings were generally not framed in Christian terms or presented as exemplifications of Christian doctrines. They were conspicuously the work of a moralist, but whether of a secular or Christian variety was not at all clear. Indeed, even a friend like Beatrice Webb always remained puzzled by Tawney in this respect, and recorded in her diary that: 'Altogether, in his religious opinions, he remains a mystery to his free-thinking friends'.[27] If Beatrice, and others, had seen Tawney's own diary, then the mystery would have been resolved. There is certainly no reason today why, in seeking to understand the basis of Tawney's thought, there should be any uncertainty on this point.

It is, of course, an important point, and more not less important because it forms the unstated inner core of Tawney's published work. It is not just that he believes in the existence of God (as a 'fact of experience'), nor in Christianity as the personification of God, revealing his nature, but that he holds these beliefs to be the indispensable basis for a true morality. If it is asked why individuals should be regarded as ends and not as means, Tawney's answer is that:

> The essence of all morality is this: to believe that every human being is of infinite importance, and therefore that no consideration of expediency can justify the oppression of one by another. But to believe this it is necessary to believe in God. . . It is only when we realise that each individual soul is related to a power above other men, that we are able to regard each as an end in itself.

Similarly, if it is asked what is the basis for a belief in human equality, the answer is the same:

> In order to believe in human equality it is necessary to believe in
> God. It is only when one contemplates the infinitely great that
> human differences appear so infinitely small as to be negligible. . .
> What is wrong with the modern world is that having ceased to
> believe in the greatness of God, and therefore the infinite smallness
> (or greatness – the same thing!) of *man,* it has to invent or emphasise
> distinctions between *men*.

These may not be the only answers, of course, but they are
certainly Tawney's. However, there is a further point which
deserves notice. Tawney may have a view of man as a species as
'only a little lower than the angels', but his view of actual men
is informed by a heavy dose of original sin. Believing that 'what
goodness we have reached is a house built on piles driven into
black slime and always slipping down into it unless we are building
night and day', he was unlikely to take an over-sanguine view
of the ease with which moral, and therefore social, advance might
be accomplished. If his work seems to give a particular emphasis
to the need for relentless efforts of will, here is surely at least
part of the explanation.

The final entry in Tawney's diary carries the date of 28
December 1914. He meditates upon 'this war', attempting to
integrate his analysis of domestic discontents with the international conflict. He finds the link in a corrupting scale of values
which fosters both Prussian militarism and industrial autocracy,
united in their confusion of power with right. The conclusion
from this is clear: 'If we are to end the horrors of war, we must
first end the horror of peace'. A further conclusion which Tawney
might have drawn from this analysis, as it was in fact drawn by
many on the Left at the time, was that the real war had to be
fought on the home front and not in 'capitalist' conflicts abroad.
Yet this was not the conclusion drawn by Tawney, either in
terms of personal conduct or political interpretation. Having

established that 'right' was being usurped by 'power' at home *and* abroad, his response was to fight on *both* fronts. It has been well said that 'the extraordinary fact about his reactions to the war was that he saw the struggle being fought out on so many levels at once'.[28] In November 1914, he enlisted in the Manchester Regiment, characteristically eschewing a commission. The final instalment of his political education was about to be completed.

This is not the place to tell the story of Tawney's war. The essential facts are easy enough to record. Soon made a sergeant, he saw intermittent action until, on the first day of the Battle of the Somme, he was hit by a shell, lay in no man's land for twenty-four hours, and came close to death. Almost the whole of his company was wiped out in the mass slaughter. His account of this experience is both a rare exercise in autobiography and a memorable evocation of a cosmic historical moment. In its compelling authenticity it strips away the rhetorical veneer that usually obscures what it really feels like both to fight and to face death in war, exposing the layers of emotional contradiction and – worst of all – the 'damnable frivolity'[29] of the whole business. It is interesting that George Orwell's account of his own similar experience in the Spanish Civil War (in his *Homage to Catalonia*) bears a striking resemblance to Tawney's 1916 essay. The hallmark of emotional and intellectual honesty is the characteristic of both.

Yet behind the facts of Tawney's war, even behind his experience of those facts, there is the more durable impact of the war on Tawney's thought. In one sense, the impact is slight. It produces no real dent in the structure of fundamental beliefs about man and society which he had put together before 1914, and his God had also survived intact. In essentials, then, the Tawney who was discharged in 1917 was the same person who had enlisted three years earlier. In another sense, though, the war may be seen to have exercised some influence. It extended his experience of working men, hitherto based either upon the experience of Whitechapel or the WEA (both perhaps unrepresentative in their own way), to include the men of the trenches. If this was a lesson in the possibilities for fellowship and collective moral purpose, it was also a lesson in the difficulties of weaning the working man from the 'selfish' philosophy he shared with his masters. In this respect a year in uniform, Tawney wrote at the end of 1915, had 'taught me a good deal'.[30]

However, this was not the most significant lesson that he wanted to bring back from the front. His real message turned on the need to close the gap between the ideals in whose name millions were fighting and dying and the social reality at home. Tawney felt this gap acutely on his return to England in 1916 and, in pressing the need to bridge it, his thought acquired both a new political urgency and a more directly programmatic focus. Addressing the England to which he and the others have returned, he offers an uncompromising rebuke: 'You make us feel that the country to which we've returned is not the country for which we went out to fight'.[31] This England had to be told that the war had changed things, that there could be no going back to the world before 1914, that 'this is a war after which there will be no Restoration'.[32] It had further to be informed that the war could only be sustained to a successful conclusion if it lived up to its ideals and became a war for social change. In the words of Tawney's famous pamphlet, the choice was between *Democracy or Defeat*.[33]

Tawney's thought at this time seems to oscillate between an excited sense of the war as having quickened the pace of social change through its radical impact upon opinion, and an angry sense of a historical opportunity being stifled and closed off. This is reflected in his discussion of economic and social issues, but especially of education, for this is 'a kind of *experimentum crucis,* an issue on which our sincerity in the causes for which we claim to have taken up arms may be brought to the test'.[34] Writing to the Master of Balliol at the end of 1917, he spoke of the country being in 'a sort of equilibrium of forces', with the war having 'caught us halfway in a transition to democracy'.[35] What Tawney was clear about in such a situation was that the issues and causes he had reflected upon and engaged in before 1914 now had to be pressed forward with again, with renewed passion and urgency, and with an even sharper sense of the need to unite moral argument with institutional reform and political action.

By the close of the Great War, then, the future pattern of Tawney's life and work is largely set. It reveals itself in the range of activities and institutions with which he was to be involved for the rest of his life. These may be briefly reviewed. There was, of course, his trio of classic books, starting with *The Acquisitive Society* (1921), moving on to *Religion and the Rise of Capitalism* (1926), culminating in *Equality* (1931), all exploring in their different ways the moral basis of social institutions and all helping to shape the process they described.[36] There was his involvement with the church, and with numerous initiatives designed to strengthen its social mission. He was a member of the Church of England Committee of Enquiry into Christianity and Industrial Problems, the report of which on *Christianity and Industrial Problems* (1918) is a thoroughly Tawneyite document. He cooperated with Temple in the Life and Liberty Movement at this same period, and later in the Conference on Christian Politics, Economics and Citizenship (COPEC) in the mid 1920s, where again his influence is apparent in the resulting reports. Throughout his life he was the constant, uncompromising voice of Anglican socialism, even when other voices (including Temple's) felt it expedient to change their tone or tune.

Equally lifelong was his educational crusade. There was the WEA of course, but much else besides. He was a prolific, relentless and frequently anonymous educational journalist, as the over-whelming dominance of educational issues in his published output of articles makes clear. From the Fisher Act of 1918 to the Butler Act of 1944 Tawney's influence is writ large over the history of educational thought and policy in Britain. He was a key figure in the landmark report on adult education of the Social Recon-struction Committee in 1919, and the central figure on the new Advisory Committee on Education established by the Labour Party in its post-1918 reorganisation. His statement of the case for *Secondary Education For All* in 1922 became the axis around which the party's approach to education revolved and 'his remained the major inter-war contribution to the formulation of its educational principles'.[37] The Hadow Report in 1926 on 'The Education of the Adolescent', a direct progenitor of the principles of the 1944 Act, was in large measure Tawney's work.

His involvement with the Labour Party, and with the wider labour movement, extended far beyond the educational field. He had returned from the war determined, through political action, to exploit the opportunities for change that the war had opened up. Thus his acceptance of a Balliol fellowship in 1918 was on the firm condition that he would be free to stand as a Labour parliamentary candidate. He stood, and lost, in Rochdale in 1918, and was equally unsuccessful elsewhere on three subsequent occasions. Along with Sidney Webb, Tawney represented the trade union side on the Sankey Commission on the coal industry in 1919, an experience which both fed directly into the arguments and examples he was assembling at this time for *The Acquisitive Society* and brought him firmly into the public eye. Beatrice Webb was not alone in thinking that Tawney, with 'his personal charm, his quiet wisdom, and his rapier-like intellect', had been 'the great success of the Commission'.[38] The Labour Party's 1928 policy statement *Labour and the Nation* came from Tawney's pen, and he also drafted its 1934 manifesto document *For Socialism and*

Peace. Behind and beyond these particular activities, he was (with Cole and Laski) a leading party theorist, as well as its stoutest friend and – at significant moments – its sternest critic. He was, in every sense, a party man.

Then there was, as if all this was not enough, his professional career as an economic historian. Appointed to a readership at the London School of Economics in 1919, he was to remain there (after 1931 as Professor of Economic History, a chair that would have come sooner but for his other activities) until his eventual retirement in 1949. In his teaching, research and writing on England in the century before the Civil War – 'Tawney's century' as it has been called – he opened up new avenues of interpretation with a boldness of scholarship and largeness of vision which won both eager disciples and no less eager antagonists. Whether his subject was the social significance of agricultural enclosures, the economic implications of Puritanism, or the rise of the social and economic power of the gentry in the period before the Civil War, the effect of his work was such that 'even those who reject his views most vigorously find themselves answering, rather than ignoring, the questions which he has raised'.[39] Of course, what was frequently at issue in these scholarly controversies provoked by Tawney's work was a larger disagreement about the proper scope of economic history and the proper role of the economic historian. Tawney's own position, most clearly and eloquently stated in his inaugural lecture in 1933, was unafraid of values, deliberately careless of academic boundary lines ('the best fish are caught when poaching'), predisposed towards large interpretations, and distinguished by an unapologetic present-mindedness. For Tawney, like his mentor in the discipline, George Unwin, economic history was at bottom a branch of moral philosophy. If this is why his approach was unlikely to find favour with those historians who 'make a darkness, and call it research',[40] it is also why his own historical work is inseparable from his other concerns.

Even this brief sketch by no means exhausts the arenas in which Tawney's presence was felt. It omits, for example, the extent to which this essential Englishman could get inside the life of other societies. Attached for a period during the Second World War to the British embassy in Washington as a labour adviser, he produced a penetrating account of the history and character of the American labour movement. Visiting China twice in the early 1930s, at the invitation of international bodies, he wrote with insight and empathy about that complex society. His *Land and Labour in China* (1932) is a minor classic. Perhaps an account of his life and work should also include mention of what he did not do, because his energies were so generously distributed and his focus always so wide. For example, the book he might have written on 'his' century is sometimes described as one of the lost masterpieces of our century.

Yet this is scarcely true to the man or his work. 'There are careers which leave on the observer an impression of consistency and completeness, as of the unconscious logic of a continuously unfolding plan'.[41] This is Tawney reflecting on the career of Lionel Cranfield, the subject of his final piece of major historical research, a career which did not leave such an impression. If not true of Cranfield, though, it is true of Tawney. He did what he wanted to do and said what he wanted to say. He may have been at his surest theoretically in the 1920s, the emphasis in his historical work may have shifted somewhat over time, but the overall impression is of a massive unity, consistency and coherence. This stretched from the personal agenda he compiled in the years before 1914 to the continued reflections on that agenda and its progress in the last years of his life (as when, Ann Oakley recalls, he 'slept cosily by our fire after Christmas dinner, and woke up to make entirely non-senile remarks and blow his yellow coltsfoot tobacco all over my mother's clean carpet').[42] He died in his sleep on 16 January 1962, in his eighty-second year. As his colleague, T. S. Ashton, put it: 'He had completed most of the tasks he had set himself in early manhood, and was not unhappy'.[43]

2 *Diagnosing the malady*

'Modern society is sick through the absence of a moral ideal'.

Social reformers, in all their variety of measures and methods, usually operate on at least two fronts simultaneously. They need, on one side, to expose and identify the deficiencies of the society which is the object of their reforming intentions; while, on another side, their task is to advance the merits of their proposed reforms. They will usually find it necessary to establish a plausible connection between the deficiencies identified and the remedies proposed, and (on a third front) to claim that there exists a method whereby the move from a defective present to an improved future may be safely accomplished. Of course, there will always be other reformers, as well as defenders of the *status quo,* who will want to offer disputatious combat on all these fronts.

The socialist critics of capitalism exemplify these characteristics. For example, those socialists who have identified the inefficiency and disorganisation of capitalism as its central defect have wanted to remedy it through a socialism of planning and order, while others, emphasising its inequalities, have wanted to advocate a redistributive and egalitarian socialism. Some socialists have indicted capitalism as a system of exploitation on scientific grounds, others on moral grounds. Some have insisted on the necessity of revolution, others on the possibility of gradual reform. It is not surprising, then, that the history of socialist arguments and traditions has been a history of both diversity and antagonism.[1] In turning to Tawney, it is useful to keep such considerations in mind, since his thought represents the most powerful version of one kind of socialist argument about the grounds upon which the social and economic order of capitalism is indicted, an alternative socialist order is proposed, and a particular method of change is embraced.

In his pre-1914 diary, Tawney had recorded his belief that what was really wrong with modern society was that it was morally 'sick'. This preliminary diagnosis was to be developed and extended in the rest of his work, most forcefully in the decade after the Great War but remaining basic to his social thought even in the decade following the Second World War. The diagnosis of society's moral sickness and the prescription for its restoration to moral health is always Tawney's central preoccupation. Frequently, and significantly, it is precisely to the medical metaphors of sickness and health that he turns in describing his theme. The first title, in its Fabian pamphlet form, of his famous 1921 book was 'The Sickness of an Acquisitive Society', and the tone and language of that original title runs through its pages. Even in 1938, writing a preface to a new edition of *Equality,* he describes the book's theme in terms of 'its analysis of the ravages of the disease of inequality, and its account of the remedies by which – would the patient consent to take them – his malady would be cured'.[2]

It is difficult to avoid seeing Tawney in the role of social doctor. Noting the symptoms, he presses on the patient the need to confront the underlying causes. His tone is concerned but uncompromising. There can be no resort to palliatives or placebos, and all quack remedies must be firmly eschewed. In prescribing a regime of vigorous moral activity, he warns of the consequences if this advice is ignored. He also knows how and when the trouble started and explains this in some detail to the patient. Society, in other words, must pull itself together and take some decisive action: 'Unless it is to move with the energetic futility of a squirrel in a revolving cage, it must have a clear apprehension both of the deficiency of what is, and of the character of what ought to be'.[3] The starting point, then, in Tawney's diagnosis is the 'deficiency of what is'.

However, in identifying this deficiency, he knows that he has a task in persuading the patient that the symptoms being experienced are attributable to what he has already satisfied himself are the root causes of the problem. Tawney has no doubt what these causes are, as the record of his 'commonplace book' makes abundantly clear. However, in preparing to convert this private analysis into a public argument, he knows that he has to persuade people who do not naturally share his own fundamental grounds, those of Christian morality, for rejecting the existing social order that the problems of the society around them are rooted in the moral inadequacy of a false philosophy. Of course, Tawney emphatically does believe that contemporary social problems are so rooted, just as he also believes that purposive social change occurs when (and because) people come to feel that the 'external' machinery of social life does not correspond with their 'internal' moral sense.[4] But this moral sense has to be constantly roused and cultivated, and this is a task he sets himself. Further, having decided as a Christian moralist that existing social and economic arrangements are, in a fundamental sense, *wrong,* he wants to persuade other people that it is because these arrangements are morally flawed that they are the scene of so much discontent and antagonism and give rise to a condition of profound malaise.

The justification for presenting Tawney's approach in this way is provided most clearly by his manuscript notes on 'The New Leviathan', almost certainly written in the period just before the composition of *The Acquisitive Society* and to be regarded as a preliminary outline for that project. Noting that 'the discontents of modern society appear mainly to be economic' (and thus become the province of assorted social reformers who 'devise particular remedies for particular ills'), Tawney responds:

But this is an error. In fact they are the result of a particular way of looking at the world, a body of assumptions and presuppositions, a philosophy. Their remedy is to be found by examining that philosophy and, if it is wrong, discarding it. That is to say they are not to be fought primarily on the economic plane at all. . . They are to be fought by seeing that economic considerations are put in their proper place in a general philosophy of life.[5]

It is the prevailing 'mechanistic' philosophy of life which is the source of social and economic ills, for across the whole of social life it has substituted 'the canon of convenience for the canon of right and wrong'. Moreover, socialists no less than individualists subscribe to it, for they too, in their preoccupation with order, efficiency and practical expediency, clearly regard society as a machine. It is a social order which, because it is seen as a 'purely human order', lacks the 'fixed points of principle' which a more eternal frame of reference would provide, as it has done in the past. Thus society is set on a failing course and even its limited successes, preventing its relapse into a complete empiricism, are 'due to the fact that we are still to a limited extent under the influence of principles given us by our history'.

Having set out his stall in this way, Tawney then adds: 'But this is strong meat. And since modern men are terrified of principles, one can introduce them to the point of view necessary to salvation by approaching the question from the existing order, and asking "How and why do our current institutions and ideas fail to satisfy the deepest parts of man's nature?"' As he runs through the reasons why men 'feel' the existing social order to be so unsatisfying, reasons which were to be developed in *The Acquisitive Society* but which turn on its failure to treat human beings *'qua* human being', the basis for Tawney's own 'feeling' about this once again emerges clearly. To believe that people should be regarded as ends and not means, so that the present relationship between worker and employer in industry becomes

31

plainly an 'immoral' relationship, this 'really involves a transcendental philosophy'. In terms already familiar from his introspections before 1914, but now with added significance as the project of public persuasion is prepared, Tawney reasserts his belief that a proper valuation of human beings depends upon them being seen as having rights beyond the arena of the temporal social order. Thus the now disparaged exponents of 'natural' rights were wrong not in what they said but in what they failed to say: 'They were right in thinking that the individual had certain rights which are absolute. They were wrong in omitting to state that the recognition of such rights implies as its basis a supernatural reference'.

Tawney's problem, and project, now emerges. How could 'modern men', enslaved by a false philosophy, be 'introduced' to the 'point of view necessary to salvation' when they no longer, except unconsciously and residually, accepted the only frame of reference within which a satisfactory social philosophy could be securely anchored? Was it necessary to win them for Christianity before they could be won for socialism? Tawney did not pose these questions so directly, but they arose naturally and inevitably from the position he had set out. It was clear why Tawney was a socialist, but why should other people who did not share his point of departure come to accept either his account of the destination to be reached or the route to be travelled?

These, then, were the questions confronting Tawney as he began to plan the task of persuading his fellow citizens that 'the cause of our troubles is to be found. . . in the fact that men have a conception of 'good' – an idea of life – a philosophy – which is inadequate'. His response to such questions might well have taken the form of an argument for the validity of Christian principles and their supernatural derivation. Significantly, this is not the form of his argument, either in *The Acquisitive Society* or *Equality,* or indeed elsewhere. Instead, his approach is twofold. On one side, he sets about the task of turning Christians into socialists (sensibly preferring this to the task of turning socialists into Christians). On another side, his aim is to persuade unbelievers of all kinds that the social problem is essentially a moral problem and that its solution is to be found in the realm of 'principles'. In undertaking this exercise in persuasion though, it was necessary to begin 'from the existing order' rather than from *a priori* positions, in order to demonstrate the relationships that were being claimed. It was necessary, in other words, to convince people from the evidence all around them that the unprecedented organisation of power in the modern world, truly a 'new leviathan', had not been accompanied by an increase in happiness and that the search for contentment demanded a radically different approach. It demanded nothing less than a return to first principles; not larger doses of a medicine which had conspicuously failed to restore a disorderly constitution, but a new prescription based upon an old and neglected formula.

All this helps to explain why *The Acquisitive Society* takes the form it does. It is presented less as an attempt on Tawney's part to persuade society of the intrinsic merits of his own moral position, with its roots in Christian doctrine, than an attempt to persuade it of the baneful consequences for its social and economic life if it continued to deal in a false philosophy. In starting 'from the existing order' in the period between 1919 and 1921, Tawney had an abundance of troubling social evidence upon which to draw, more even than in its preface in the 'unrest' before 1914. Stephen Spender describes how a turn-of-the-century feeling of being 'a fortunate promontory of time towards which all other times led' was replaced, as a result of the Great War, by a profound anxiety: 'The war had knocked the ball-room floor from under middle-class English life. People resembled dancers suspended in mid-air yet miraculously able to pretend that they were still dancing. We were aware of a gulf but not of any new values to replace old supports'.[6] The year in which *The Acquisitive Society* was published was also the year in which Britain probably came closer to a serious revolutionary upheaval than at any time in its modern history. Morally and psychologically, industrially and politically, British society seemed to be coming apart at the seams.

This, then, was the social order from which Tawney started. Reminding his readers that 'there are times which are not ordinary', he could plausibly address them as 'a nation which has stumbled upon one of the turning points of history' when 'the broken ends of its industry, its politics, its social organisation, have to be pieced together after a catastrophe'.[7] However, before reconstruction there had to be deconstruction, before action there had to be reflection. The broken ends could not be put right until there was a proper understanding of what had gone wrong. This understanding was not helped by those who either recommended higher doses of the same medicine or, in their desire to do something, confused symptoms with causes. The former included those who ('like parrots') repeat the cry of 'Productivity' as the basis for a reconstruction of economic life 'regardless of the fact that productivity is the foundation on which it is based already, that increased productivity is the one characteristic achievement of the age before the war. . . and that it is precisely in the century which has seen the greatest increase in productivity since the fall of the Roman Empire that economic discontent has been most acute'. The latter included those who regarded poverty and its alleviation as the major social problem, without understanding that 'poverty is a symptom and consequence of social disorder, while the disorder itself is something at once more fundamental and more incorrigible'.

In Tawney's view, the fundamental source of the social disorder and malaise was to be found in the absence from social and economic life of 'a common body of social ethics'. The effect of this was that there were no widely accepted rules of conduct and no basis for a unity of effort. The system, in other words, lacked legitimacy. Without a basis in real authority, it could only rely upon power, and this was not a durable basis for a social or economic system. The appeals for more cooperation in industry were bound to fall on deaf ears because cooperative effort in shared objectives was not a principle upon which industry was organised. Unless and until society decided to seek that 'which maketh men to be of one mind in a house' (one of Tawney's favourite Biblical borrowings), it would continue to be afflicted with all the disruptive consequences of a house divided against itself.

This is Tawney's central, relentless theme. He exemplifies and illuminates it from a number of directions. In particular, in an enterprise he was to make his own, he sketches the historical process whereby the dissolution of a former stock of social ethics took place. The combined forces of secularism and liberalism had removed from social thought the idea of social purpose or common social ends, replacing it with a privatised and mechanistic view of social life. Church and state 'withdrew from the centre of social life to its circumference', leaving the field formerly occupied by a conception of common ends to be occupied merely by 'private rights and private interests, the materials of a society, rather than a society itself'. Economic life had formerly been regarded as one branch of the moral life of the whole society, but in the new dispensation had been declared a moral-free zone. In shaking itself free, properly so, from the zealotries and tyrannies of priests and kings, the modern world had achieved one kind of emancipation, but in the process had delivered itself into the hands of a philosophy which destroyed the basis for *any* common social purpose by emancipating economic activity from the realm of moral regulation.

35

Societies in which this philosophy held sway could, argued Tawney, be called 'acquisitive' societies, since 'their whole tendency and interest and preoccupation is to promote the acquisition of wealth'. Rights are divorced from the performance of functions, the absolute sanctity of private property is affirmed, and the unrestricted pursuit of economic self-interest is the ruling ethos. A society of this kind has taken the moral brakes off: 'It assures men that there are no ends other than their ends, no law other than their desires, no limit other than that which they think advisable. Thus it makes the individual the centre of his own universe, and dissolves moral principles into a choice of expediencies'. Such a society was not without its attractions, as Tawney freely acknowledged. Its ideology of possessive individualism appealed to a powerful human instinct. It simplified social life by removing the need for ethical discrimination between different kinds of economic activity. It was also a motor of economic expansion, such that having achieved an output per head of around £40 by 1914 'it is possible that by the year 2000 it may be doubled'.

Why, then, could not such a society, along with the philosophy which sustained it, be regarded as a durable historical achievement? Tawney's answer was that it had brought with it 'a group of unexpected consequences' which were the cause of its current malaise. Moreover, these consequences were not accidental but derived from its essential nature. An acquisitive society might set its sights on unlimited economic expansion, but even while it was extending its outworks the nature of its operations had set in motion a series of corrosive fractures in its foundations. Lacking any principle to regulate the acquisition of wealth, it had opened the way to an irrational inequality based not upon opportunity, energy or service but upon the power of property. In this situation, even the wealthy lost their self-esteem, for as the recipients of functionless incomes their wealth was not sanctified by a social purpose. Certainly the rest of the population was degraded, and felt this degradation, because 'the admiration of society is directed towards those who get, not towards those who give; and though workmen give much they get little'. It was not surprising, then, that an acquisitive society lacked contentment and happiness.

There were other consequences too. In its massive inequality, it misdirected production away from the needs of the mass of the population to the superfluities demanded by the 'small class which wears several men's clothes, eats several men's dinners, occupies several families' houses, and lives several men's lives'. Much of what was produced was not really wealth but waste (an echo here by Tawney of Ruskin's 'illth' and Morris's 'shoddy'), while urgent needs went unmet. The existing misdirection of production was the real question to be put to those who simply clamoured for 'more' production: 'Produce what? Food, clothing, house-room, art, knowledge? By all means! But if the nation is scantily furnished with these things had it not better stop producing a good many others which fill shop windows in Regent Street?' Yet this question had no meaning in a society which had abandoned any principle by which to evaluate economic activity beyond the market expression of economic power.

Then there was the further consequence of such a society that 'social life is turned into a scene of fierce antagonisms, and that a considerable part of industry is carried on in the intervals of a disguised social war'. There was much lamentation about the industrial strife, yet such conflict was inevitable since there was no shared interest between the different 'sides' of industry and no principle by which rewards could be assessed. If the only rule of economic activity was the vigorous pursuit of self interest, then it was hardly to be expected that this would provide a reliable recipe for industrial peace. If there was no principle of limitation, then the sky was the limit. It was as pointless to expect government intervention to be successful in this situation ('as though the absence of a principle could be compensated by a new kind of machinery') as it was to look to an increase in national wealth to act as a solvent to a problem which was not about amounts but about proportions. An acquisitive society was, by its very nature, a society of industrial discord.

It was also a society in which the false philosophy which ruled its economic life had spread out to contaminate the whole of the rest of social life. Instead of being merely one part of the general life of a society, necessary but subsidiary, economic preoccupations had been inflated and elevated to the point where they dominated and coloured all other activities. Here was a society in the grip of 'fetish worship', and this particular fetish was described by Tawney as 'industrialism', likening it to the militarism which had become the Prussian fetish. 'The essence of industrialism', he explained, was:

> not any particular method of industry, but a particular estimate of the importance of industry, which results in it being thought the only thing that is important at all, so that it is elevated from the subordinate place which it should occupy among human interests and activities into being the standard by which all other interests and activities are judged. When a Cabinet Minister declares that the greatness of this country depends upon the volume of its exports, so that France, which exports comparatively little, and Elizabethan England, which exported next to nothing, are presumably to be pitied as altogether inferior civilisations, that is Industrialism. It is the confusion of one minor department of life with the whole of life.

In its confusion of means with ends, it was an authentic expression of a society without a common purpose. Like international society, to which it bore a striking resemblance, it was a realm of power without authority, of claimed rights without acknowledged duties. The fate of such a society, both internationally and domestically, was already evident: 'What we have been witnessing. . . during the past seven years, both in international affairs and in industry, is the breakdown of the organisation of society on the basis of rights divorced from obligations. Sooner of later the collapse was inevitable, because the basis was too narrow'.

In examining the insecure basis of domestic society, Tawney gave particular attention to the institution of property and the organisation of industry. The rise of passive, functionless property had stripped private property of much of its traditional justification. Divorced from work or function, it was now to be regarded (in J. A. Hobson's term) as 'improperty'. Its purpose was acquisition and power; its consequence was the class inequality and division which characterised and defaced contemporary society. Thus the 'agreeable optimism' which regarded these darker aspects of social life as mere 'excrescences', capable of being removed by further economic progress, will 'not survive an examination of the operation of the institution of private property in land and capital in industrialised communities'. Tawney was conducting his own examination of the operation of private property in the coal mining industry at this time, as a member of the Sankey Commission, an experience which is abundantly reflected in the range of examples deployed in *The Acquisitive Society,* just as the book's general argument about functionless property is deployed to assail the witnesses who came before the Commission (like the mining engineer, who, having asserted the property rights of the owner, has to acknowledge the fairness of Tawney's restatement of the owner's royalty as 'simply payment for a private right quite irrespective of any function which is performed or any work that is done').[8] In its modern form, private property ownership is firmly identified by Tawney as the source of society's most acute maladies. Lacking a secure moral basis it generates gross inequalities, wields a power over people's lives comparable at times to that exercised by feudal lords, promotes class divisions and class warfare, and makes impossible the achievement of either real efficiency or social peace.

The organisation of industry is the arena where these consequences of functionless property are most clearly manifest, equally damaging to the interests of consumers and producers. Consumers suffer because there is no 'community' interest by which to measure the claims of producers, for 'before the community can be exploited, the community must exist, and its existence in the sphere of economic relations is today not a fact, but only an aspiration'. Producers suffer because they are merely the 'labour' or 'hands' of functionless property, not partners in a common enterprise. Moreover, these are not abstract considerations, for Tawney argues that the basis upon which industry is organised is in the process of breaking down. It is a breakdown of motivation for 'the instruments through which capitalism exercised discipline are one by one being taken from it'. Less passive and more educated, workers are no longer driven to work through fear of unemployment or starvation and are no longer prepared to accept their status within an industrial autocracy. What this means is that capitalism can no longer justify itself as an engine of effort and efficiency, its central claim, since the basis for this is itself now being eroded. All economic systems rest upon a motivational basis of some kind and this is now the terrain where capitalism is vulnerable and defective: 'For the matter at bottom is one of psychology. What has happened is that the motives on which the industrial system relied for several generations to secure efficiency, secure it no longer'. Thus even on the grounds of efficiency, authority and discipline (and Tawney's socialism, unlike some others, is very concerned with such matters), the deficiencies of the present industrial system are increasingly evident.

This, then, is the case which Tawney assembled against the Acquisitive Society. It was presented as a society afflicted with a systemic disease, to which all its significant symptoms of illness and dysfunction could be traced and attributed. Lacking a secure foundation in a common body of social ethics, it had replaced functions by rights and social purpose by private interest. It was a community in name only. Released from moral restraints, economic life had both generated vast inequalities and swollen to deform the general life of society. Because the social order was organised around principles of self-interest rather than common interest, it had its foundation in a principle of division not of unity. It was, therefore, scarcely surprising that such a society carried with it a range of troubled consequences, not the least of which was that its economic life was 'in a perpetual state of morbid irritation'. It was, literally, a society in the grip of a civil war which, even when contained and suppressed, rumbled along beneath the surface of its social and economic life, sapping its energies, and spasmodically breaking through with increasing severity into open conflict. It was a society dominated and undermined by 'an embittered struggle of classes, interests and groups', and a continuous war of this kind 'must, sooner or later, mean something like the destruction of civilisation'.

Such was the uncompromising diagnosis pronounced by Tawney to his anxious contemporaries. Its form, to emphasise the point again, was significant. He delivered not an abstract moral sermon, pressing his own values, but an argument for moral reconstruction closely tied to a wide-ranging, abundantly illustrated, and historically informed analysis of the troubled condition of contemporary society. If this is the sort of society you want, he seems to be saying, then you should at least know what its consequences are. When he came to argue the case for *Equality,* the same approach was in evidence. Not merely was equality morally necessary, but it was also necessary if the debilitating ravages of a society afflicted by the 'disease' of inequality were to be remedied. Indeed, Tawney's argument is always conducted on these two fronts. On one side, his analysis of contemporary society is designed to indict its assorted inequalities as morally offensive, because human beings (*qua* human beings) should not be treated like that. However, on a second front, in case the response to his argument is that this sort of society is *preferred,* then while accepting this statement of moral preference (usually with a remark about not being able to argue with 'the choice of a soul') he wants to demonstrate that such a perverse moral preference is not without its consequences for the life of those societies in which it is practised.

In *Equality,* therefore, Tawney offers a dual analysis of what is wrong with English society (which is not, of course, to suggest either that there is any doubt about which kind of analysis he regarded as primary or about the genuineness of his belief in the connection between them). In presenting an analysis of the character of inequality in England, he wanted to identify its moral inadequacy. As he described the cumulative inequalities of both condition and power in a society so dominated by the 'religion of inequality' that it deserved anthropological investigation, he pressed the deficiency of such arrangements when set against the test of moral values. Here was a society in which not just material circumstances but education, health, freedom, choice, culture, and even life itself, was measured on a scale of class inequality: 'The destiny of the individual is decided, to an extent which is somewhat less, indeed, than in the past, but which remains revolting, not by his personal quality, but by his place in the social system, by his position as a member of this stratum or that'.[9] It was morally revolting that education should be divided by class, that the distribution of income and capital was so unequal, that the poor died earlier than the rich, that working class life was riddled with insecurity, that the fate of millions should be determined by the power of a plutocratic few, that industry should be organised as an autocracy, that a political democracy was also a social oligarchy. As Tawney compiled his indictment of what was wrong with English society, there could be no doubt that what he intended to describe was a moral malady requiring a moral response.

However, there is a further point here to be noticed. If his argument was that the nature of inequality was morally 'revolting', he did not seek to ground such revulsion merely in his own Christian position. Instead, and interestingly, he invoked the values of a generalised 'humanism', arguing that the different senses in which the term was used were really the 'different dialects of a common language'. It was not the property of a sect but the common possession of a civilisation. It was not the antithesis of religious belief, but of materialism:

> Its essence is simple. It is the attitude which judges the externals of life by their effect in assisting or hindering the life of the spirit. It is the belief that the machinery of existence – property and material wealth and industrial organisation, and the whole fabric and mechanism of social institutions – is to be regarded as means to an end, and that this end is the growth towards perfection of individual human beings.

It was against this test that a society distinguished by severe and capricious inequalities was to be judged morally defective. Such a society offended against a view of humanity which was the noblest and most significant product of our civilisation. It was in this sense that Tawney could describe such a society as uncivilised, and expect to be understood.

If this was an argument about moral inadequacy, there was also an argument about social inadequacy. Taking his text from Matthew Arnold, Tawney wanted to suggest not merely that inequality was anti-humanist but that a society founded upon it was likely to break down. Arnold had been right to stress the practical consequences of inequality, even if today he would be 'less impressed by inequality as a source of torpor and stagnation, and more by inequality as a cause of active irritation, inefficiency and confusion'. In describing, and indicting, the nature of inequality in England, Tawney wanted to identify not merely its moral defects but its social and economic effects. In the first edition of *Equality* (which, although published in 1931, was the product of a 1929 lecture series), the main emphasis was directed towards the debilitating and divisive social consequences of the situation it described. Social and economic inequality, of both condition and power, prevented society from achieving the fruits of social unity and solidarity. It could not build a common culture, the basis for cooperative energy, because of the divisive social attitudes it generated. It could not diffuse a general well-being throughout society, because it paid less attention to common needs than to the privileges which 'drive a chasm' across social life. It was, in essentials, a society of social distance rather than of social cohesion, and therefore failed to achieve those benefits which flowed from the cultivation of the latter.

Indeed, not merely did a society of this kind fail to achieve benefits, but it inflicted upon itself severe disabilities. Social and economic inequalities served to 'clog the mechanism of society and corrode its spirit'. They also served as the motor of social antagonism organised on class lines:

> Except in so far as they are modified by deliberate intervention, they produce results surprisingly similar to those foretold by the genius of Marx. They divide what might have been a community into contending classes, of which one is engaged in a struggle to share in advantages which it does not yet enjoy and to limit the exercise of economic authority, while the other is occupied in a nervous effort to defend its position against encroachments.

Writing the preface to a new edition of *Equality* in 1938, and doubtless responding to the economic circumstances of that desperate decade, Tawney sought to underline the economic relevance of his argument against those who might believe that the 'morally repulsive' could be defended on the grounds that it was also the 'economically advantageous'. He advanced four reasons why social and economic inequalities 'so far from being an economic asset. . . are an economic liability of alarming dimensions'. They misdirect production, away from necessaries and towards unnecessaries. They fail, because of this neglect of basic necessities, to cultivate the human energies needed for productive activity. They sustain vested interests which hamper the task of economic reconstruction. Finally, they give rise to a permanent class struggle which prevents constructive cooperation. The conclusion was clear: 'Whatever the ends which these features of our society may serve, economic efficiency is certainly not among them.'

Lecturing to a WEA class during the early days of the Second World War, with equality as his subject, Tawney reported that when he had written on this theme a decade earlier 'the considerations which influenced me were the effects of capricious inequalities on the quality of English social life'. He had written out of a sense of 'indignation'; it had been 'a protest on behalf of human dignity'. However, he now felt that the balance of the argument could be put rather differently: 'While the case against inequality on grounds of justice appears to me as convincing as it always was, the case for it on grounds of national unity and strength seems to me more convincing'.[10] In speaking in this way (and, of course, the wartime context is clear), perhaps Tawney underestimated the extent to which his original argument was conspicuously an argument about the conditions for social unity and community, and the strength to be derived from the cultivation of these attributes. Just as it had also been an argument about the conditions for social contentment and happiness:

Social well-being does not only depend upon intelligent leadership; it also depends upon cohesion and solidarity. It implies the existence, not merely of opportunities to ascend, but of a high level of general culture, and a strong sense of common interests, and the diffusion throughout society of a conviction that civilisation is not the business of an elite alone, but a common enterprise which is the concern of all. And individual happiness does not only require that men should be free to rise to new positions of comfort and distinction; it also requires that they should be able to lead a life of dignity and culture, whether they rise or not, and that, whatever their position on the economic scale may be, it shall be such as if fit to be occupied by men.[11]

Enough has been said to demonstrate that when Tawney marshalled his case against the social and economic order of his day, he wanted to identify both its moral deficiency and the practical consequences of a society organised around such a deficiency. He was a moralist certainly, but also a robustly practical one. If, on one front, his charge against the existing social order was that it was not 'fit to be occupied by men', this moral charge drew support, on a second front, from a wide-ranging analysis of the practical difficulties experienced by a society distinguished by such moral unfitness. This was the form of his argument in both *The Acquisitive Society* and *Equality*. Tawney's social medicine had established an intimate connection between moral and physical health or sickness, and the derivation of the latter from the former. If his diagnosis centred on the moral problem of values, it also gave much attention to the practical problem of 'expediences' (as he frequently described the world of means rather than of ends). Society suffered from a moral disorder, associated with its lack of a common stock of social ethics and reflected in the functionless, inegalitarian character of its social and economic life. This moral disorder, and the society built upon it, necessarily brought with it a range of undesirable consequences. It could not achieve either social or industrial peace, nor the economic progress which depended upon the energy of cooperative effort. It is, perhaps, worth stressing, if only because the charge is often made, that Tawney's position did not involve the repudiation of the goals of economic efficiency and growth, but (among other things) a sustained statement of the superior contribution to these goals of an economy based upon cooperative effort rather than upon competitive self-interest. On this, as on the other matters here, Tawney's argument may or may not be well founded. For the moment, though, it is sufficient to record that this was his argument.

There remains a further dimension of Tawney's diagnosis of moral and social malaise which requires notice, not least because it formed one of his major (and distinctive) preoccupations. He was concerned to explore not only the nature and consequences of society's moral sickness, but also the source and development of the malady. If society lacked what it had once possessed, namely a body of social ethics, and if this deficiency was identified as its central failing, it was relevant to ask how such a lamentable condition had developed. This was a question to which Tawney devoted considerable attention. In both *The Acquisitive Society* and *Equality* he was concerned to frame his argument within a discussion of 'the historical background' (as a chapter title in the latter book described it). The aim was to demonstrate how, at a certain period and associated with new social forces, a social philosophy was developed which was at once both emancipatory and partial. In attacking legal and political privilege, it had nothing to say about social and economic privilege: 'It condemned the inequalities of the feudal past; it blessed the inequalities of the industrial future'.[12] It erected a *cordon sanitaire* around economic life, protecting it from general moral inspection and denying the existence of a social ethics with a writ extending across the whole terrain of social and economic life. Ethical life had been privatised.

Against this background, Tawney's particular concern was to explore how this revolution in social philosophy had been accomplished and the nature of the resistance to it. Significantly, the final pages of *The Acquisitive Society* assert both the essentially 'religious' character of the doctrine it advances and the shameful retreat from this doctrine of the Christian churches who should have been its most strenuous defenders and advocates: 'The abdication by the Christian Churches of one whole department of life, that of social and political conduct, as the sphere of the powers of this world and of them alone, is one of the capital revolutions through which the human spirit has passed'.[13] Tawney's special mission was to investigate the circumstances of this abdication. His focus was the process whereby Christian doctrine had retreated from a general social ethics to a position of 'indifferentism', relegating itself to the sphere of private conduct and disavowing any larger moral authority in the life of society. This was not, of course, a matter of purely historical interest.

It should be recalled that, when Tawney began seriously to work this historical seam in the 1920s, he was actively engaged in a range of initiatives aimed at strengthening the social gospel and role of the Anglican Church. It was a period when the climate for such initiatives seemed unusually favourable. Thus Tawney's historical work fused both with his analysis of the moral defect at the core of contemporary society and with his engagement with an agency whose proper task was the repair of that defect. He began to read widely and deeply in the history of Christian social doctrines. One fruit of that reading was his wife's edition of Baxter's *Christian Directory* (1925), the introduction to which showed many marks of Tawney's own hand and passages from which were to be reproduced almost *verbatim* in his famous work of the following year. Richard Baxter's 1673 book, in which the Kidderminster preacher sought to 'establish the rules of a Christian casuistry, which may be sufficiently detailed and precise to afford practical guidance to the proper conduct of men in the different relations of life, as lawyer, physician, schoolmaster, soldier, master and servant, buyer and seller, landlord and tenant, lender and borrower, ruler and subject',[14] was to be seen as a textbook of Christian social ethics. It served both as a powerful reminder of a great tradition and as a striking example of how, even when it was written, it had already been subsumed by the rising tide of indifferentism.

One issue, in many respects the most significant of all, on which traditional doctrine had collided with developing practice was that of usury. This became, therefore, a particular subject of Tawney's attention. In 1925 he produced his celebrated edition of Thomas Wilson's *Discourse Upon Usury* of 1569, prefaced by a book-length introduction which was not only a scholarly account of credit and capital in the sixteenth century but also an explicit attempt to situate Wilson's argument, delivered by the Preacher to the Lawyer and the Merchant, within the same venerable tradition of Christian social thought. It was 'the tradition of men so different as More and Starkey and Latimer, whose social philosophy was based ultimately on religion, and who saw in the economic enterprise of an age which enclosed land and speculated on the exchanges, not the crudities of a young and brilliant civilisation, but the collapse of public morality in a welter of disorderly appetites'.[15] If Wilson's argument about usury had lost out, even by the end of the sixteenth century, it was nevertheless important to record that he and others 'did not surrender without a struggle'. As in his earlier study of the enclosure controversy in *The Agrarian Problem in the Sixteenth Century,* Tawney wanted to focus on the clash of opinion provoked by economic change. Even more so than enclosure, the struggle over usury went beyond the particular issue itself and involved the status of a whole scheme of social ethics:

For the theory of usury which the sixteenth century inherited had been not an isolated freak of casuistical ingenuity, but one subordinate element in a general system of ideas, and the passion which fed on its dusty dialectics is intelligible only when it is remembered that what fanned it was the feeling that the issue at stake was not merely the particular question, but the fate of the whole scheme of medieval economic thought which had attempted to treat economic affairs as part of a hierarchy of values embracing all human interests and activities, of which the apex was religion.

In attempting again to fan the historical flames of this particular controversy, Tawney also intended to direct attention to the general tradition of Christian social thought from which it derived and, thereby, to throw further light on one source of contemporary problems.

He approached this task even more directly when he delivered the first series of Scott Holland Lectures in 1922. The general rubric of the lectureship was 'the religion of the incarnation in its bearing on the social and economic life of man'; and Tawney chose as his subject 'Religious Thought on Social Questions in the Sixteenth and Seventeenth Centuries'. It was several years later, in 1926, that the substance of these lectures was published as *Religion and the Rise of Capitalism*. His theme may have been historical, but his purpose was explicitly contemporary. The separation of Christian ethics from social and economic life had been the hallmark of the nineteenth century, but 'the boundaries are once more in motion' and 'issues which were thought to have been buried by the discretion of centuries have shown in our own day that they were not dead, but sleeping'.[16] In examining the structure of medieval social ethics, the breakdown of that structure in the sixteenth century, and the role of Puritanism in facilitating that breakdown, Tawney was seeking to draw attention to issues which he believed were central to an understanding of contemporary, twentieth-century malaise. The sixteenth century was the cockpit where the new forces and ideas, replacing organism by mechanism, social responsibility by individual responsibility, social ethics by private ethics, met with resistance from 'a great body of antithetic doctrine'.[17] Tawney's aim, in part, was clearly to re-establish the historical credentials of that body of Christian social thought. However, his further aim was to indict that tradition for its failure to modernise its doctrines to take account of the new problems presented by a developing capitalism. Hence these doctrines 'were abandoned because, on the whole, they deserved to be abandoned. The social teaching of the Church had ceased to count, because the Church itself had ceased to think'. Reduced to the status of 'piety imprisoned in a shrivelled mass of dessicated formulae', the social theory of the Church 'was neglected, because it had become negligible'.

Here, then, was an essential element of Tawney's analysis of social and economic ills. A traditional social ethics, able to give purpose and unity to social life, had been overturned by new forces and new doctrines. This was a revolution with consequences which 'have been worked into the very tissue of modern civilisation'. Some of these consequences, like the material conquest of nature, had been exhilerating. Yet, because 'the most obvious facts are the most easily forgotten', there had also been consequences of a different kind: 'Both the existing economic order and too many of the projects advanced for reconstructing it break down through their neglect of the truism that, since even quite common men have souls, no increase in material wealth will compensate them for arrangements which insult their self-respect and impair their freedom'. The neglect of this truism was the central error of the social philosophy of the modern age, just as the understanding of it was the central contribution of both an older social philosophy and of socialist critics of capitalism. It defined the essential source of the contemporary social malaise:

It is that whole system of appetites and values, with its deification of the life of snatching to hoard, and hoarding to snatch, which now, in the hour of its triumph, while the plaudits of the crowd still ring in the ears of the gladiators and the laurels are still unfaded on their brows, seems sometimes to leave a taste as of ashes on the lips of a civilisation which has brought to the conquest of its material environment resources unknown in earlier ages, but which has not yet learned to master itself.

With this analysis of the historical genesis of a false social philosophy, Tawney's diagnosis of the nature of the social problem was complete. The problem was essentially a moral one, but this moral disorder set in motion a train of social and economic disorders. Thus Tawney's diagnosis combined an argument about the moral deficiency of capitalism and the system of ideas which sustained it with a second argument, capable of being heard even by those who were morally deaf to the first, about the practical disabilities necessarily suffered by a society without a sound basis in social ethics. Lacking such a basis, a capitalist system of property relations had established itself which was 'the magnetic pole which sets all the compasses wrong'.[18] For Tawney, of course, the moral argument was always primary, even if it drew support from an argument about consequences. What was wrong with capitalism was that it was *wrong*. It was rooted in a view of human beings as means and not as ends. Having framed this moral diagnosis in the 1920s, Tawney continued to advance it for the rest of his life. Thus when, in the 1930s, the socialist case seemed to turn on the breakdown of capitalism, he wanted to declare that it was 'not its breakdown but its existence'[19] which was the problem. When, in the 1950s, the socialist case seemed to turn on the economic vitality of capitalism, he maintained the view that it rested upon 'a decision that certain types of life and society are fit for human beings and others not'.[20] Thirty years earlier he had identified 'the problem of moralising economic life'[21] as the central issue; and that always remained the problem to which he addressed his considerable moral and intellectual energy.

3 Prescribing the remedy

'As a society sows, so in the long run it reaps'.

When *Religion and the Rise of Capitalism* came to be reviewed in the *Times Literary Supplement,* the reviewer rightly identified its purpose as part of a project aimed at 'respiritualising our civilisation, especially in economic life'.[1] However, the sense in which this was Tawney's project has to be tied to his critical commentary in that book on the failure of just such a spiritual tradition in the past. It had failed, at a decisive moment, to adapt its doctrines to meet the challenge presented by new social and economic forces. Instead of developing its scheme of social ethics in response to the structural transformation in the character of finance, capital and economic organisation, religious social thought continued to treat economic transactions as categories of personal conduct until, finding this approach ignored as irrelevant, it abdicated from social and economic life altogether.

This historical failure is the indispensable background to an understanding of Tawney's definition of the contemporary task. It was not enough to seek a remedy for modern ills by dusting off the long buried formulae of the past. That was mere antiquarianism. The real task certainly involved restoring the idea and the pedigree of a general body of social ethics, but such a restoration would only succeed (or, at least, have a chance of succeeding) if it directed its practice and its application towards the problems presented by the nature of the contemporary social and economic order. A new social philosophy had an old one upon which to draw, both in terms of the definition of its proper scope and of the moral categories (such as those of social purpose, function and equal worth) with which it worked. It represented, even if it did not achieve, 'the magnificent conception of a community penetrated from apex to foundation by the moral law',[2] the only durable solution to the problem of social unity and social peace. Yet, starting from this basis, a new social philosophy was required to restate these older conceptions and categories in terms of their relevance to the capitalist organisation of economic life. For it was *that* kind of economic order which now needed to be remoralised.

Tawney's programme has to be seen in this light. If it was a moral programme, its cutting edge had to be severely practical. His was a moralism which carried with it a ferocious contempt for the kind of windy moral rhetoric, whether in politics, education or the church, which was all puff and no push. One incident during Tawney's time as a tutorial class teacher provides a nice example of his general attitude. When Mansbridge showed him a proposal for a collection of essays on adult education, back came the angry reaction that the suggested authors would 'produce merely pious platitudes about how nice it is for people to be educated. . . not only useless but debauches the mind. . . typical of the worst kind of Dilletantism. . .'[3] In all the arenas within which he was actively engaged, such as the WEA, the Labour Party and the church, Tawney remained a relentless critic of the pious platitude as the substitute for either rigorous thought or vigorous action. An abstract moralism of good intentions was, decidedly, not enough. Indeed, it was often an obstacle in the path of something more bracing and effective. Contrary to an image of him that has sometimes been cultivated, Tawney – as both man and social thinker – was nothing if not unsentimental.

It was in this spirit, then, that he approached the task of remoralising social and economic life. In his major books of social philosophy, he set out to demonstrate what was involved in the application of a social ethics to the social and economic structure of capitalism. It certainly involved the moralist in getting his hands dirty, by taking some trouble to understand the nature of the material world rather than merely treating it with either moral anger or a lofty moral disdain. The task required 'a cool head as well as a stout heart', for 'common sense and a respect for realities are not less graces of the spirit than moral zeal'.[4] In this sense, at least, involving a recognition of the importance of social facts and economic knowledge, it could perhaps be described as a Fabian enterprise (acknowledged in the dedication of *Equality* to the Webbs). In another sense, though, the nature of the task to be undertaken involved an approach that was profoundly unFabian. Just as there were socialists who offered a faulty diagnosis of society's malady, failing to understand that the moral inadequacy of an entire social philosophy was at issue, so there were those who, for this reason, were the purveyors of inadequate and ineffective remedies. In his notes on 'The New Leviathan', Tawney had identified the problem: 'Most of the Reformist or Revolutionary movements, which attack the existing order, themselves accept, without realising it, the assumptions of that order.'[5]

However, the particular subject of Tawney's remarks here was 'a certain school of socialists' who did realise, because they liked to proclaim the fact, that their new society would 'grow insensibly out of existing arrangements'. What these socialists seemed to want was a social order with more organisation and tidiness than the present one: 'They appear to think that the evils of the existing order can be removed by leaving it as it is and heaping regulation upon regulation to check its abuses'. Operating with an inadequate conception of human nature, socialists of this kind might claim that their purpose was the extension of human freedom but their practical proposals indicated their continued attachment to an instrumental view of human beings. Thus they 'appear to conceive the best life for most men as one in which they are regimented by experts'. If these remarks were clearly directed against a prevailing Fabianism, in its classical Webbian form, Tawney was to have occasion to direct similarly critical remarks against the prescriptions offered, and applied, by other false socialisms. In particular, of course, it became important to refute the view that the 'police collectivisms' which were the singular contribution of official Marxism to the twentieth century provided a path for socialists in the West to follow. Such a view was 'either ignorance or a credulity so extreme as to require, not argument, but a doctor'.[6]

Tawney frequently commented upon the diversity of socialism. It was a term which bristled with 'radiant ambiguities'.[7] This made it necessary to define and distinguish the kind of socialism that was being discussed or recommended. If Tawney did not put the matter quite so directly, this was implicit in the character of his argument. It was reflected in his reservations about an 'ethical' socialism which lacked any practical bite; a 'practical' socialism which was innocent of any larger, transformative purpose; a revolutionary romanticism which was 'all rhetoric and blank cartridges';[8] and an undemocratic socialism which was contemptuous of 'bourgeois' liberties. There is a strong undercurrent of differentiation in all of Tawney's socialist arguments, separating good socialist doctrines from bad ones, the essential from the inessential, values from mechanisms, ends from means. There is also a strong sense of an argument being conducted, deliberately and self-consciously, within the setting of a particular cultural tradition, sensitive to the nuances of time, temper and place. In declaring that socialism must 'wear a local garb', he believed that 'a socialism which is to exercise a wide appeal must be adapted to the psychology, not of men in general, nor of workers in general, but of the workers of a particular country at a particular period'.[9] On a number of counts, then, Tawney has to be seen as recommending a certain *kind* of socialism, even when (as in his claim that the 'impulse' behind British socialism has always been 'obstinately and unashamedly ethical')[10] associating that kind with the attributes of a more general tradition.

Thus Tawney did not merely offer 'socialism' as the antidote to the malady afflicting contemporary civilisation, but a socialism of a distinctive kind. Having established that the real source of the malady was to be located at the level of 'principles', he sought to establish the credentials of a number of key principles, currently neglected or denied, and to demonstrate what was involved in their application to social and economic life. Three principles in particular stand out from his argument, each illuminating a field of issues. They may be described as function, freedom, and equal worth. It is necessary to say something about each of these in turn, before discussing the claimed effect of their combined application.

The idea of function has a complex and elusive history in the realm of political thought. It has served as a principle both of unity and of differentiation. It has sustained an authoritarian politics and also a libertarian politics. Its role has been centralist and corporatist, but it has also been decentralist and pluralist. Moreover, these divergent uses were much in evidence when Tawney was writing his *The Acquisitive Society,* the central theme of which turns on the antithesis between an acquisitive and a 'functional' society. They were particularly in evidence in the guild socialist movement, which proposed that industry should be conducted by self-governing guilds developed out of the trade unions, and to which Tawney was attached (as an active member of the National Guilds League while writing *The Acquisitive Society*). If one kind of 'functional' guild socialist argument (represented best by Ramiro de Maeztu's *Authority, Liberty and Function* in 1916) pointed towards a corporatist authoritarianism, another kind (best represented by the work of G. D. H. Cole) was designed to lay the basis for a pluralistic liberty. The key issue was the nature of the relationship between associational life and the state (with industry, of course, regarded as a major assoication).

Tawney's usage of the idea of function did not follow either of these paths. Instead, drawing upon medieval conceptions of a social unity grounded in common moral purpose, and upon a tradition of social and cultural criticism of industrial capitalism of the kind expressed by Ruskin's 'there is no wealth but life', he advanced the idea of function as the characteristic idea of a society imbued with a social purpose, a society of common ends. Function belonged to a vocabulary of service, duty, and obligation, the language of a society unified by a social purpose and rooted in a body of social ethics. Tawney defined its meaning, with industry as his leading example:

> A function may be defined as an activity which embodies and expresses the idea of social purpose. The essence of it is that the agent does not perform it merely for personal gain or to gratify himself, but recognises that he is responsible for its discharge to some higher authority. The purpose of industry is obvious. It is to supply man with things which are necessary, useful, or beautiful, and thus to bring life to body or spirit. In so far as it is governed by this end, it is among the most important of human activities. In so far as it is diverted from it, it may be harmless, amusing, or even exhilarating to those who carry it on; but it possesses no more social significance than the orderly business of ants and bees, the strutting of peacocks, or the struggles of carnivorous animals over carrion.[11]

Modern society had replaced purpose by mechanism, functions by rights, a principle of unity by a principle of division. The task, then, was to reverse this process, with all its disagreeable consequences, by restoring a purposive conception to social life. In so far as this restoration of social purpose was achieved, then the principle of function would be established as the cornerstone

59

of social and economic life. It would define activities in terms of
their contribution to a general social purpose. But what was this
social purpose? What were the common ends around which a
social unity was to be constructed? Tawney, it seems, was less
concerned to answer such questions than to rehabilitate the *idea*
of social purpose, for it was this which had become lost. Perhaps,
as his *Commonplace Book* had suggested, he believed that common
ends were readily available in the moral traditions of society and
required only the will to be established and enforced. They did
not need to be invented, merely to be revived.

What Tawney was concerned to demonstrate, however, was
the radical implication of applying the idea of function to property, industry and economic activity. Even without specifying
the common ends of society as a whole, it was possible to suggest
that industry had a purpose beyond the satisfaction of the acquisitive appetites of those who engaged in it. Drawing upon a long
and varied tradition of social thought, Tawney could argue that
'the principles upon which industry should be based are simple,
however difficult it may be to apply them' and these principles
were that 'its function is service, its method is association'.[12]
Once it was established that the purpose of economic activity
lay in meeting the economic needs of society (and what else
could its purpose be?), then it was possible to assess particular
activities, roles and institutions in terms of their contribution to
this end. In other words, they could be evaluated in terms of
their function:

> A society which aimed at making the acquisition of wealth contin-
> gent upon the discharge of social obligations, which sought to pro-
> portion remuneration to service and denied it to those by whom
> no service was performed, which inquired first, not what men
> possess, but what they can make or create or achieve, might be
> called a Functional Society, because in such a society the main
> subject of social emphasis would be the performance of functions.[13]

It was in this sense that much of the economic life of modern society was, literally, functionless. The fact that it was sometimes argued that the pursuit of private interests also served, as an agreeable by-product, to satisfy general economic interests, or that private economic rights yielded to considerations of public interest at times of national emergency, confirmed rather than refuted this verdict. The essential principle of modern economic life turned on an assertion of economic rights and the denial of economic obligations. Having identified the dire social and economic consequences of this false philosophy, Tawney went on to advance the merits of a society with function instead of rights as the basic principle of its economic life. In doing so, he was not content with a general statement about the superiority of a purposive and ethically based approach to economic matters, but wanted to show what was practically involved in the reconstruction of contemporary economic life upon the basis of function.

It involved a radical alteration in the nature of property ownership. If function was used to discriminate between legitimate and illegitimate forms of property, then much of modern property had to be regarded as essentially functionless. Deprived of the justifications traditionally provided by the historical theories of property ownership, it was reduced to the assertion of a 'right' independent of any function it served. In fact, much property had to be regarded not as a right but a privilege, for 'the definition of a privilege is a right to which no corresponding function is attached'.[14] Tawney's argument at this point is impressive, certainly within the socialist tradition, both for its demonstration of the inadequacy of historical theories of property in the face of the transformed character of property ownership under capitalism and for its careful unpicking of the different forms of property in a way which enabled the functional and the legitimate to be separated from their opposite. Much of private property stood condemned less by the arguments of socialists than by the application to the modern world of the traditional defences of private property ownership. Further, the real opposition was revealed not as that between private and public property but between the functional and the functionless. If functionless ownership should be abolished, then functional ownership of various kinds should be encouraged. This policy, therefore, was favourable to the extension of appropriate forms of both public and private ownership:

> For it is not private ownership, but private ownership divorced from work, which is corrupting to the principle of industry; and the idea of some Socialists that private property in land or capital is necessarily mischievous is a piece of scholastic pedantry as absurd as that of those Conservatives who would invest all property with some kind of mysterious sanctity. It all depends what sort of property it is and for what purpose it is used.[15]

Thus the principle of function applied to the modern economy suggested that private ownership should be abolished where, as in most of the major industries, the private owner was the functionless and absentee shareholder, but that it should be encouraged in those areas of economic activity where the worker-owner was appropriate. Indeed, a socialist policy would not only extend the 'property' as this term was understood by the vast majority of the population, but would actively seek to extend and diffuse many kinds of legitimate property ownership. 'Whatever the future may contain', writes Tawney, 'the past has shown no more excellent social order than that in which the mass of the people were the masters of the holdings which they ploughed and of the tools with which they worked, and could boast, with the English freeholder, that "it is a quietness to a man's mind to live upon his own and to know his heir certain"'.[16] This was not an appeal to the past (although a significant indication of the spirit

in which Tawney approached these matters) but an argument
for the modern application of the functional principle which
underpinned traditional forms of property-holding. Functionless
property had squeezed out these older forms of property ownership over much of economic life, an example of bad property
driving out good, and those (like the 'distributivists' associated
with the ideas of Belloc and Chesterton) who wished to restore
small property ownership in industry and agriculture should
therefore regard the extinction of functionless property as an
indispensable preliminary.

Yet this was not an approach appropriate to the major industries which dominated economic life. Here the principle of function demanded the abolition of the existing functionless form of
private ownership, but left open the question of the method by
which this was best accomplished. Just as Tawney refused the
simple antithesis between private and public ownership at the
level of principle, so he also asserted the scope for a considerable
flexibility in the method and form whereby industries might be
released from the yoke of functionless ownership. Indeed, once
this yoke was removed, then it would be possible to disentangle
the variety of elements of which property was composed and to
redistribute these in many different forms of detailed ownership.
All this was a matter of 'expediency', not of fundamental principle,
and could be decided in terms of individual cases. Thus nationalisation (that 'singularly colourless word') should properly be
regarded as 'merely one species of a considerable *genus* . . . a
means to an end, not an end in itself'.[17] Its role was to end the
private ownership of industry, where this was necessary, not to
inaugurate the management of industry by the state. In this sense
it was an enabling measure. There was a problem of language here:

It is an unfortunate chance that English-speaking peoples employ
one word to express what in France and Germany are expressed

63

by two, *étatisation* or *Verstaatlichung* and *socialisation* or *Sozialisierung,*
– words which in those languages, unlike the common English
practice, are used, not as synonyms, but as antitheses – and that
no language possesses a vocabulary to express neatly the finer shades
in the numerous possible varieties of organisation under which a
public service may be carried on.[18]

There could and should be variety in the organisational and
financial structure of public services, with different forms of
administration, consumer representation and producer involvement. Tawney describes these matters as a problem of 'constitution-making' and argues for the vigorous exercise of constitutional imagination in approaching them. However, there is a
further sense in which constitution-making had to be undertaken,
deriving from a second principle which Tawney brings to his
prescription for the restoration of social and economic health.
This is the principle of freedom. If functionless property was one
source of the social problem, then arbitrary power was another.
Tawney has a strong sense of capitalism as a system of unequal
economic power. Defining power, in words which anticipate a
usage made familiar by modern political scientists, as 'the capacity
of an individual, or group of individuals, to modify the conduct
of other individuals or groups in the manner which he desires,
and to prevent his own conduct being modified in the manner
in which he does not',[19] he is able to extend the discussion of
the question of power and responsibility from the political system
– where it is usually confined – to the wider terrain of social
and economic life.

In general, Tawney treats political freedom in Britain as an
accomplished fact, the product of a successful democratic revolution achieved by constitutional means. Even though he can be
found criticising 'our habit to talk. . . as though political democracy was fully established in this country' as an 'illusion', certainly
in the absence of effective control of election spending, the

abolition of the House of Lords and electoral reform on the basis of the 'transferable vote',[20] he was not (unlike, say, G. D. H. Cole) a general critic of British political arrangements. In essentials, the British political system met the requirement that political power should be accountable and responsible. Moreover, political freedom was important, even supremely important, as Tawney felt obliged to point out to those socialists who, in their devotion to economic emancipation, seemed to overlook this inconvenient truism: 'The truth is that a conception of Socialism which views it as involving the nationalisation of everything except political power, on which all else depends, is not, to speak with moderation, according to light. The question is not merely whether the State owns and controls the means of production. It is also who owns and controls the State'.[21]

Both political and economic freedom were important. Moreover, both were to be seen as part of the general problem of social power. If political freedom in Britain was largely an achievement of the past, then the achievement of economic freedom remained a task for the present and the future. Capitalism was a system of concentrated and irresponsible economic power. The organisation of industry was essentially tyrannical, involving the exercise of arbitrary power and the denial of freedom to the worker. The inequality which characterised a capitalist society was not just a matter of economic circumstance and condition, but also a matter of power. For all these reasons, then, the question of freedom was at the centre of Tawney's socialist prospectus. It had informed his approach to an anti-poverty strategy when, in 1913, he had stressed the need to strengthen the 'economic resisting-power' of working people in order to nourish a non-dependent freedom. It informed his discussion of measures aimed at reducing social inequality and extending social welfare, for such measures were extensions of practical freedom for the vast majority of the population. It informed his argument about the kind of 'constitution' required by an industry after the removal of functionless private ownership. It informed his analysis of the need to constitutionalise economic power which was presently irresponsible.

The task, then, on different sides, was to curtail arbitrary power and extend freedom. Perhaps two aspects of Tawney's argument for freedom deserve emphasis. First, there is the attempt to carry the case against arbitrary power from the political realm to the economic. This attempt ran up against the tendency to regard freedom 'as belonging to human beings as citizens, rather than to citizens as human beings'.[22] If understandable in historical terms, this was a misguided and partial view of the problem of power, since it was quite possible for a society to be 'both politically free and economically the opposite'. It may have succeeded in bringing irresponsible political power to democratic heel, while still allowing untamed economic power to roam free in the jungle. Thus what was lacking was 'the economic analogy of political freedom', which meant that 'the extension of liberty from the political to the economic sphere is evidently among the most urgent tasks of industrial societies'. If a person's freedom as a consumer was mocked by monopoly economic power, or freedom as a worker mocked by autocratic management and the financial power of functionless owners, then the claim that such a person was free because free as a citizen was itself a mockery. It rested upon a misunderstanding of the nature of both power and freedom.

The connection between power and freedom is the second aspect of Tawney's argument to be noticed. If not a power (because that, on his own definition, involved an ability to change the conduct of others), freedom was certainly relative to power. Arbitrary power of all kinds had to be curtailed if freedom was to flourish. In that sense, it was appropriate to think in terms of freedom *from* tyranny (though, of course, not only of political freedom from the state). In another and more positive sense, however, it was appropriate to think of freedom not as a position to be defended but as a 'capacity' to be strengthened and extended. Its essential quality was not negative but positive, active not passive, concrete not abstract, plural not singular. It was the freedom *to* act, choose, live. It consisted in the 'opportunity for self-direction'.[23] All this became clear once it was recognised that 'liberty is composed of liberties'.[24] Freedom was not an exhibit in the museum of political concepts, but a practical capacity of everyday life: 'It means the ability to do, or to refrain from doing, definite things, at a definite moment, in definite circumstances, or it means nothing at all'.[25] Because freedom had this character, social and economic policies designed to extend collective provision and reduce inequality were also properly to be seen as effecting a redistribution of freedom. It was perverse, even though a perversity in wide political currency, to claim that the extension to the nation of a possession of a class involved a general contraction of freedom. Since 'the majority of ordinary men are not born with financial and social winds behind them', to such people freedom was necessarily seen 'less as a possession to be preserved than as a goal to be achieved'.[26] Thus a social and economic policy which converted the privileges of the few into the opportunities of the many was 'twice blessed', for it 'not only subtracts from inequality, but adds to freedom'.[27]

If Tawney's argument here, as elsewhere, was concerned to make the case for freedom in terms of social policies to extend collective provision and equalise opportunities in education, health and housing, of taxation policies to redistribute income and wealth, of industrial policies to strengthen the position of the worker, and of economic policies to bring the power of private capital under public direction, this did not exhaust the ambitions of his argument. Indeed, there remained a further matter of considerable importance. This concerned the organisation of freedom, its 'constitution', both in industry and in the wider society. Freedom involved the diffusion of power and the direct exercise of responsibility. It required that power should be responsible, devolved and accessible. Thus when Tawney discussed the 'liberation of industry' he meant both its liberation from functionless private ownership and its conversion into an arena of active, practical freedom for those engaged in it. The objective was to end arbitrary power, not to replace its private form with a public version: 'If industrial reorganisation is to be a living reality, and not merely a plan upon paper, its aim must be to secure not only that industry is carried on for the service of the public, but that it shall be carried on with the active co-operation of the organisations of producers'.[28]

Tawney's answer to the question of how this aim was to be achieved was contained in his proposal that industry should be treated as a 'profession'. In making this proposal he was not innocent of the self-regarding aspects of professional bodies, but wanted to stress that combination of self-government and public service which was the essential idea of a profession. It was precisely that combination of freedom in service which should characterise the organisation of industry, extending to all those who worked in it. This was the difference between the existing organisation of industry, the collectivism widely proposed as its replacement, and the professionalisation of industry: 'The first involves the utilisation of human beings for the purpose of private gain; the second their utilisation for the purpose of public service; the third the association in the service of the public of their professional pride, solidarity and organisation'.[29] The second was an improvement upon the first and might well have much of the same machinery as the third, but only the latter reflected a view of freedom as involving a sufficient devolution of power to enable the assumption of collective responsibility. Although Tawney first framed this argument in the wake of the Great War, when the movement for industrial democracy was in full cry, a quarter of a century later he was still denying that this movement had been 'a transient emotional disturbance'[30] and continued to maintain that the demand contained within it would have to be met in some form if the organisation of industry was to satisfy basic human aspirations, of which the aspiration for freedom was the most basic of all.

As was seen in his use of the idea of function, Tawney's discussion of industrial freedom made him a somewhat idiosyncratic (if, for a time, quite active) member of the guild socialist movement which had this as its central issue. Describing himself on one occasion as 'though possibly an unorthodox guild socialist, and certainly disagreeing with some of its exponents', he welcomed the guild movement because it 'brings English socialism out of the back waters and bypaths of government regulation, in which it was boring itself ten years ago, into the mainstream of the socialist tradition, which has as its object not merely the alleviation of poverty, but an attack on the theory of functionless property'.[31] However, in giving his own understanding of guild socialism as the 'conduct of industry by professional organisations for the public service', it was clear why he differed from some of its exponents. In particular, he could not share the 'sectionalism' of the functional democracy advocated by Cole, the leading guild theorist, with its erosion of the role of a supreme authority. Tawney was certainly in favour of the diffusion of power. His early notes on 'The State and Minor Associations' agreed with the view that 'the acute question of the future is the relation between the state and minor associations'.[32] His argument for public ownership was accompanied by an insistence on its decentralised diversity: 'When Birmingham and Manchester and Leeds are the little republics which they should be, there is no reason to anticipate that they will tremble at a whisper from Whitehall'.[33] Yet the reviewer of *The Acquisitive Society* in the journal of the guild socialist movement was correct in seeing Tawney as 'thinking along his own lines and quite independently' (though, happily and significantly, arriving at guild conclusions). Tawney was a guild socialist who was not also a pluralist. Moreover, unlike Cole, his emphasis is less upon the assertion of democratic rights and more upon the assumption of profess-ional responsibilities.

It will be necessary to return to this matter, because it illumin-ates much in Tawney's general position. However, it is more immediately necessary to turn to the third axial principle which underpins his socialist argument and programme. This is the principle of equal worth. Although discussed last, there is every reason to regard it as primary. As the evidence provided by his *Commonplace Book* clearly revealed, this was the inner core of his whole structure of personal and social morality, the rock of Christian principle upon which everything else was based. In this sense, it was a rock of faith and not of philosophical argument. It was the expression of religious-based traditions of thought about human beings and their worth which were 'articles of faith not susceptible of proof by logic'.[34] Since all men were the children of God, each was infinitely precious, an end not a means, rich in the possibilities for self-development, brothers and sisters in a shared humanity and a common civilisation. This is what is described here as Tawney's principle of equal worth. Either this view of human beings was taken, he seemed to say, or it was not; but either way it had to be seen as a moral decision, replete with social consequences. 'I judge men', he once remarked, 'mainly by whether [they are] equalitarians'.[35] When he applied his principle of equal human worth to the structure of English society, his judgement was delivered not in the measured language of the social philosopher but in the angry tone of the outraged moralist. Human beings, on universal perspective, were both infinitely great and infinitely small, but this overwhelming commonality (not in doubt 'when their clothes are off') was thwarted in practice by 'the whole odious business of class advantages and class disabilities, which are the characteristic and ruinous vices of our existing social system'.[36] Such an arrangement was an affront both to men and to their maker.

In describing Tawney's principle as that of 'equal worth', instead of a more familiar 'equality', it becomes easier to get inside the texture of his argument and to integrate its various strands. It identifies it as a particular *kind* of argument for equality, and as an argument for a particular *kind* of equality. Tawney's equality is concerned with a 'spiritual relation', and its essential theme is that: 'Because men are men, social institutions – property rights, and the organisation of industry, and the system of public health and education – should be planned, as far as is possible, to emphasise and strengthen, not the class differences which divide, but the common humanity which unites, them'.[37] Because men are men: at every point Tawney's argument is anchored in that simple statement of fundamental moral truth. It implied a relational equality, an equality of relationships in a society where people were within 'reach' of each other. In a class society distinguished by severe social and economic inequalities, people were out of reach of each other and society became, not the social affirmation of a common humanity which it should be, but the scene of social division, antagonism and injustice.

On the one hand, then, Tawney wanted to show what the principle of equal human worth implied for social and economic arrangements. It implied that there should be equality of access to the 'means of civilisation', both physical and spiritual. Burke's maxim that all men have equal rights but not to equal things was trumped by the fact that

> unfortunately, Nature, with her lamentable indifference to the maxims of philosophers, has arranged that certain things, such as

light, fresh air, warmth, rest and food, shall be equally necessary to all her children, with the result that, unless they have equal access to them, they can hardly be said to have equal rights, since some of them will die before the rights can be exercised, and others will be too enfeebled to exercise them effectively.[38]

There could be no justification for the division of the physical means of life on class lines. Indeed, most chilling and chastening of all, there was the ultimate intolerability of a class division in life and death chances: 'The poor, it seems, are beloved by the gods, if not by their fellow-mortals. They are awarded exceptional opportunities of dying young'.[39] Nor could there be unequal access to education and culture, the spiritual means of civilisation. For Tawney, education was always the touchstone for the values of a society and, for this reason, he reserved his fiercest prose for the class pyramid of educational provision in England, with the public schools as its apex of privilege, and for the valuation of human beings which this system represented. A system which tied education to wealth was a 'barbarity' and demanded thoroughgoing reconstruction: 'The English educational system will never be one worthy of a civilised society until the children of all classes in the nation attend the same schools. Indeed, while it continues to be muddied by our absurd social vanities, it will never even be efficient as an educational system'.[40] On all these fronts, then, Tawney was able to pursue the radical implications for social and economic policy of the principle of equal worth.

On the other hand, though, his argument was also concerned to identify what this principle and its application did *not* imply. It did not imply a policy aimed merely at equalising 'opportunities', for in the absence of a foundation of practical equality that was an illusion: 'As though opportunities for talent to rise could be equalised in a society where the circumstances surrounding it from birth are themselves unequal!'[41] Indeed, worse than illusory, it was also 'the impertinent courtesy of an invitation offered to unwelcome guests, in the certainty that circumstances will prevent them from accepting it'.[42] Yet this was not the most significant reason why 'equality of opportunity' was flawed. Its practical failure was rooted in the moral inadequacy of its valuation of human beings, with its emphasis on the ladder of opportunity for the few but neglect of the needs of the many. Tawney christened this 'the Tadpole Philosophy', a view of life in which, like the chance for a small minority of tadpoles to become frogs, the condition and needs of all were regarded as secondary to the opportunities available to a few. Such a view of life was not compatible with the principle of equal worth.

However, this principle did not imply a mathematical equality of reward or treatment either. Treating people equally was not the same as treating them identically. People had different needs, which should be met in appropriately different ways (like a mother, as Tawney suggests in one of his familiar Socratic arguments by analogy, who attends to the different needs of her children by devoting particular care to those with the greatest needs). Nor did it imply an identity of reward, since there were good grounds (on the principle of function) for differential rewards for service performed. What mattered was to end the differences between classes which stood in the way of a common civilisation, not to erode differences of treatment or reward between individuals. The latter would lose its social and psychological significance when the former was accomplished:

> What is repulsive is not that one man should earn more than others, for where community of environment, and a common education and habit of life, have bred a common tradition of respect and consideration, these details of the counting-house are forgotten or ignored. It is that some classes should be excluded from the heritage of civilisation which others enjoy, and that the fact of human fellowship, which is ultimate and profound, should be obscured by economic contrasts, which are trivial and superficial. What is

> important is not that all men should receive the same pecuniary income. It is that the surplus resources of society should be so husbanded and applied that it is a matter of minor significance whether they receive it or not.[43]

Thus remaining inequalities would have lost their sting.

Tawney's equality as equal worth should also be distinguished from two further kinds. The first is that espoused by the moralist as implying an equality of 'consideration', involving either no very clear implications for policy or even sometimes implications of a decidedly inegalitarian variety. Tawney, by contrast, was always emphatic about the need not merely to enunciate a moral position in general terms but to show its practical implications for the social and economic world: 'A common culture cannot be created merely by desiring it. It must rest upon practical foundations of social organisation'.[44] When Archbishop Temple consulted Tawney on the wisdom of appending a practical programme to his *Christianity and Social Order,* the advice received was that it 'adds a note of realism'.[45] It was always an important part of Tawney's argument that the failure to reconstruct society on a sound moral basis was a moral refusal, and had to be seen as such, not presented as a consequence of the practical difficulties involved. What he described as the 'strategy of equality' involved a range of measures which were 'the most familiar of commonplaces'.[46] The failure to implement them was a moral choice, not a practical dilemma. A second kind of argument to be distinguished from Tawney's is that of the philosopher (of whom John Rawls is the leading contemporary example) who constructs a case against 'unjustifiable' inequalities on the basis of a calculus of interest plausibly undertaken by people without knowledge of their place in the social system and of a calculus of the social advantages and disadvantages of particular inequalities. This may be a good case, made even stronger and more radical by further glosses on it, and with consequences for an attack on unjustified inequalities similar to Tawney's. Yet this is not Tawney's case, which is relational not calculative, rooted in equal worth not in distributive justice, socialist not liberal. The attempt to derive justice from 'expediency' was precisely what Tawney did *not* do. His appeal was not, as with Rawls, to a 'difference' principle but to a principle of fellowship and solidarity. It was also, of course, an appeal not to the categories of the philosopher but to the moral sense of everyman.

These, then, were the central principles which Tawney brought to the task of 'respiritualising our civilisation'. Not content to state them in general terms, he identified their implications for the organisation of social and economic life. Function implied a radical alteration in the basis of property and industry. Freedom demanded a new organisation of power. Equal worth meant a society without class differences. Yet these were not separate principles, but the interlocking elements of a conception of a purposive moral community. They have been separated and disentangled here, but in Tawney's hands they are always firmly integrated and mutually sustaining. Thus function struck a blow against functionless inequality and opened up arenas of functional freedom. Freedom expressed itself in functional service and addressed the inequality of power. Equal worth nourished a practical freedom and drew upon function as a criterion of reward. From first to last, the seamlessness and unity of Tawney's argument is striking, along with the comprehensiveness of its range and ambitions. These characteristics were expressions of the kind of argument it was, in which diagnosis and prescription were united by their source in an unwavering moral analysis of the troubled condition of contemporary society.

However, an account of Tawney's reconstructive principles, and of their practical application, cannot stop there. A further, indispensable aspect of his argument remains to be identified. This turns on the alleged consequences for the life of society of the principles and programme he recommends. Just as his diagnosis of the malady of modern society combined an argument about moral sickness with an attribution to this source of the most significant social problems and discontents, the symptomatic social consequences of a fundamental moral disorder, so his prescriptive remedy for this condition was not confined to an identification of a superior moral medicine but carried with it a powerful claim about the beneficial consequences to be expected from its administration. In both diagnosis and prescription, an argument about moral health is indissolubly connected to an argument about social health. A good society could only be constructed upon a sound moral basis.

But what was a good society? Although Tawney had his own answer, he seems to suggest that on *any* plausible view of the ingredients of a satisfactory social order the application of his programme of moral reconstruction had a contribution to make. People were free to make good or bad moral choices, but they were not free to choose the consequences of these choices. It was not even the case, notwithstanding his perennial stress on the need for a revaluation of the place of economic activity in the life of society, that the economy would flourish best under competitive rather than cooperative conditions. Tawney was not prepared to allow even that hostage to ideological fortune, although it was the case that: 'Even if the way of cooperation did not yield all the economic advantages expected from it, we should continue to choose it. Both the type of individual character and the style of social existence fostered by it are those which we prefer.'[47] This should, perhaps, be read alongside his famous dictum that: 'As long as men are men, a poor society cannot be too poor to find a right order of life, nor a rich society too rich to have need to seek it.'[48] This was not, of course, an argument that it mattered little whether a society was rich or poor, still less that there was a trade-off between prosperity and rightness, but in fact formed part of his case that, in twentieth century conditions, continued economic progress depended crucially upon getting a 'right order of life'. It was not the reason for seeking to get it, nor a reason to abandon the search if its economic fruits turned out to be disappointing, but it was to be seen as a probable and plausible consquence.

If this is emphasised, it is because Tawney is sometimes presented as happily exchanging economic goods for moral goods. In fact, not only did he not make an exchange of that kind, but offered an account of the conditions in which economic efficiency and industrial production would be enhanced. What he did argue, however, was that a society which had a creed of possessive individualism as its dominant ethos, which regarded economic activity as an end and not as a means, would never achieve either tranquillity or contentment, for it contained within it no principle of limitation. It was necessarily a society of permanent dissatisfaction, rooted in a restless and insatiable acquisitivism, incapable of producing either individual contentment or social peace. Here was the link with the 'type of individual character' and 'style of social existence' which provided the real grounds upon which a social order and the body of ideas which sustained it should be judged. These were the grounds upon which the reconstruction of society was most necessary, and where the benefits from such reconstruction would be most evident and profound: 'The fundamental question, after all, is not what kind of rules a faith enjoins, but what type of character it esteems and cultivates'.[49] An acquisitive and competitive capitalism fostered one type of character. A socialism of right relationships and school of social ethics would foster another.

More important, then, than the economic gains to be expected from new motives, functional service, professional freedom and

77

the redirection of production, there were the gains to be expected in terms both of individual and social character. Social and economic activities would acquire meaning and significance as functional contributions to a common purpose. The extension of freedom gave new scope for self-development. The erosion of class inequalities enabled a common culture to develop and released both individual and social energies. Here we arrive at the heart of Tawney's claim for a remoralised society and a major preoccupation of his thought. It is the claim that

> in spite of their varying characters and capacities, men possess in their common humanity a quality which is worth cultivating, and that a community is most likely to make the most of that quality if it takes it into account in planning its economic organisation and social institutions – if it stresses lightly differences of wealth and birth and social position, and establishes on firm foundations institutions which meet common needs and are a source of common enlightenment and common enjoyment.[50]

It is the claim that 'it is the mark of a civilised society to aim at eliminating such inequalities as have their source, not in individual differences, but in its own organisation, and that individual differences, which are a source of social energy, are more likely to ripen and find expression if social inequalities are, as far as practicable, diminished'.[51] It is the claim that social well-being requires a foundation of social cohesion and solidarity, which only a common culture can provide.

In short, it is a claim about the quality of social life. It is also central to Tawney's whole argument, not a gloss upon it. Indeed, his case for a functional society, or for an egalitarian society, can be read as subsidiary and instrumental elements in the construction of a conception of social unity, cohesion and integration. This would be a misreading of his position, although accurate in its perception of the centrality of his concern for a social unity rooted in common moral purpose and of his emphasis on the social disorder and malaise inherent in a society without such a foundation. Yet it would be a misreading nevertheless, for what is significant about Tawney's position is the *combined* nature of his argument for moral health and social health. On the one hand, fellowship is a moral expression describing a proper valuation of human beings. On the other hand, it is a description of the quality of social relationships to be found in a society built upon that valuation. The important point is that, for Tawney, it was *both* of these things. When, in 1951, he came to add a new chapter to *Equality,* he had to take account not only of the equalising trends of the 1940s but the attacks on those trends in the name of liberty, diversity, vitality and culture. He took the attacks seriously, for the names they invoked were important and they challenged his own claims about the benefits to be gained from a more equal society. In meeting this challenge, unpicking the arguments and assembling the evidence, he pitted Eliot (equality as cultural poison) against Arnold (equality as cultural tonic). On the evidence so far, his verdict was that Arnold was ahead.

4 Ends and means

'In the West there are means without ends; in China ends without means'.

It is already clear that Tawney had much to say on both the ends and means of politics, and on the nature of their relationship. The theme is basic to his work, as historian and as social moralist, reflected in his usage of a language of 'ends' and 'means' which provides the characteristic idiom within which almost all his arguments are set. He clearly believed that a proper grasp of these matters was an indispensable attribute of social understanding. It is important, then, to elucidate this organising concept of his work, in its several aspects, and to discuss something of what it involved. If, on one side, it involved a general moral argument, it also, on another side, provided the basis for a particular recommendation about the appropriate strategy for socialists in Britain.

The terrain encompassed by this theme has been glimpsed, from different angles, at various points in the preceding discussion. It was sharply apparent in Tawney's pre-1914 diary, with its suggestion that it should be possible to construct a general political agreement about 'fundamental' values and confine political disagreement to secondary and instrumental matters, thereby combining social unity of 'conduct' with diversity of 'opinion'. It was evident in his indictment of modern society for so organising its economic and social affairs that it committed the 'ultimate and unforgivable wrong' of dividing mankind into 'those who are ends and those who are means'.[1] It was seen from another direction in his discussion of the status of public ownership in the socialist argument as essentially that of 'means'. It was abundantly visible in his construction of a case for equality upon the basis of an argument about what was implied in the equal valuation of human beings as 'ends'. What such examples reveal (and many others could be cited) is not only that Tawney relied heavily on this general theme in all his work, but also that he drew upon it in a number of different ways. The first task, therefore, is to clarify some of the leading senses in which he deployed the vocabulary of ends and means.

There are, perhaps, five main usages in evidence. These may be briefly identified, before discussing some of their implications. First, there is the matter of common ends. A central thread of Tawney's work is concerned with the 'endless' condition of contemporary society, the consequences of this deficiency, and the need to remedy it. This provides the major theme of *The Acquisitive Society* and of all his formative reflections. The modern period had witnessed the replacement of a conception of public ends by a doctrine of private means, representing the dissolution of social purpose without which a society could achieve neither unity nor direction. Mechanism without purpose, means without ends, this was the enervating disability at the core of the social problem. The restoration to society of a conception of common ends, able to give meaning and purpose to the activities and machinery of social life, was therefore an essential and urgent political task.

Second, there is the affirmation as the fundamental principle of personal and public morality that people should be treated as ends and not as means. This principle was flouted on all sides in the existing organisation of social and economic life, from the class division of education to the autocratic basis of industry. If taken seriously, as a positive doctrine of equal worth, it necessitated a radical reconstruction of the landscape of social and economic life, as the argument of *Equality* was designed to demonstrate. Capitalism was characterised by 'its subordination of human beings to the exigencies, or supposed exigencies, of an economic system, as interpreted by other human beings who have a pecuniary interest in interpreting them to their own advantage'.[2] Furthermore, it was this subordination, the failure to treat all human beings as ends, which was the real source of the dissatisfaction with capitalism as an economic system:

> The revolt against capitalism has its sources, not merely in material miseries, but in resentment against an economic system which dehumanises existence by treating the mass of mankind, not as responsible partners in the co-operative enterprise of subduing nature to the service of man, but as instruments to be manipulated for the pecuniary advantage of a minority of property-owners.[3]

This instrumental treatment of human beings was wrong, was felt to be wrong, and was incompatible with any morally satisfactory form of social organisation.

Third, there is the emphasis on the importance of not confusing means with ends in discussing projects of social reconstruction. It was necessary at all times to distinguish the primary matter of the ends towards which proposals were directed, thereby defining their essential nature, from the secondary matter of the particular methods and machinery by which these ends were to be realised. The former raised issues of principle, the latter merely issues of expediency and technique. Both were important, but not equally important:

> Organisation is important, but it is important as a means, not as an end in itself; and, while the means are debated with much zeal and ingenuity, the end, unfortunately, sometimes seems to be forgotten. So the question which is fundamental, the question whether the new organisation, whatever its form and title, will be more favourable than the old to a spirit of humanity and freedom in social relations, and deserves, therefore, that efforts should be made to

establish it, is the object of less general concern and less serious consideration than the secondary, though important problem, which relates to the procedure of its establishment and the techniques of its administration.[4]

The failure to make this distinction was a source of much confusion, not least when issues which turned fundamentally on different conceptions of ends were treated as involving only questions about means. This was relevant for an understanding of the past as well as for an analysis of the present. Thus the difference between the viewpoint of a sixteenth-century peasant and a modern economist on the agrarian revolution of that period was 'not one of methods only but of objects, not of means but of ends'.[5]

Fourth, there is the need to be clear about the ends of all political activity and public policy, by which they must always be judged. The same was true of political doctrines, and 'the only sound test of a political doctrine was its practical effect on the lives of human beings'.[6] It was not what was claimed but what was delivered that mattered. However, the test of practical effect on the lives of individual human beings had to be consistent with a proper valuation of the nature, needs and potentiality of human beings. Thus the whole 'machinery of existence' had to be regarded and assessed in terms of its contribution to an end which was 'the growth towards perfection of individual human beings'.[7] The fundamental point here was that: 'The spiritual energy of human beings, in all the wealth of their infinite diversities, is the end to which external arrangements, whether political or economic, are merely means'.[8] This was the end, in the form of a practical humanism, against which policy and practice had constantly to be measured and evaluated.

Fifth, there is the importance of means as political method. It was necessary, in a general sense, to ensure that the methods employed were fully integrated with the ends to be achieved, both in terms of strategic effectiveness and of the values common to both. It was a standing danger of political life, confirmed by contemporary experiences, that 'the means destroy the end'.[9] These considerations were relevant to British socialists in framing a political strategy, and this was the matter to which chief attention had to be paid. Such a strategy for British socialism had to be rooted in a domestic political culture, thoroughly democratic, bold in vision and resolute in action. When it failed in any of these particulars, it had to be instructed firmly in the path of methodological righteousness. A conception of political ends was thus tied, at least in the British case, to a no less clear conception of the appropriate political means.

These, then, in outline, are the main senses in which Tawney deploys a vocabulary of ends and means in constructing his position. Each illuminates a significant dimension of his work, while together (and, although separated here, they are woven into the unified texture of his thought) they span much of what is distinctive and important about Tawney's social analysis. Having briefly identified their essential features, the task now is to bring them into broader focus by examining some of their implications and, where this seems to be the case, some of the problems and difficulties associated with them. There are things to be said and questions to be asked under each of the heads identified here.

This is certainly so with the matter of common ends. Enough has been said already to indicate how central this was to Tawney's thought. He had a painful sense of the lack of social unity around a common purpose and shared values in modern society, and a pressing sense of the need to see the building of socialism less in terms of the machinery of social change and more in terms of the construction of a scheme of social ethics able to supply the unity and cohesion that came from agreed ends. This theme, approached from different angles and drawing other arguments in support, has been noticed as a crucial strand running through all his major works. It also appears as a shaping influence on some of his more subsidiary concerns. An interesting example of this is provided by the reports he produced on China, following his visits there in the early 1930s. The warm sympathy towards China which Tawney displayed ('a world which has excited his curiosity and won his affection'[10]) derived above all from his feeling for the spiritual unity of Chinese civilisation. He likened this, significantly, to the unity of medieval Christendom, the dissolution of which had provided the starting point for his own historical and social analysis, in being 'the unity of a civilisation rather than of a political system'.[11] Its foundation was a common ethical code, not the machinery of law or politics:

> In culture and spirit, she has possessed for many centuries a unity more profound than that of some societies whose governmental machinery is more highly centralised. In no country is the impression of a nation, not merely as a territorial unit or a political system, but as a living personality, more insistent and irresistible. The sane policy is not to impair that unity, but to find means of extending it from the cultural sphere to that of political organisation.[12]

The West had much to teach China about the 'machinery' of life, but much to learn from China about the 'art of living'. However, such a neat reciprocity needed a rider:

> The machinery is useless or destructive in the absence of a philosophy of life to control and direct it. The West staggers blindly for lack of one, helpless amid powers it is unable to use. It cannot give to the East what it does not possess. Itself bewildered and confused, it can bring to China, in the realm of ideas, little but uncertainty and confusion.[13]

Tawney's message, then, was that China could only find the 'dynamic' it needed by building upon the 'historical culture' of its own civilisation.

If China had a problem of means, the West had a more fundamental problem of ends. In developing this theme, Tawney's account of China can be seen to complement his account of the breakdown of a medieval ethical order. Both illuminated the lack of common ends in modern society, one from a historical perspective, the other from a comparative vantage point. In each case, of course, we learn much not only about history or about China, but also about Tawney. The same is true of his treatment of other matters, where a concern with the achievement of a social unity rooted in common ends usually lurks just beneath the surface of his argument. It exercised a decisive influence on his account of, and attachment to, the working class movement, for 'the idea of social solidarity. . . is the contribution of the working classes to the social conscience of our age'.[14] Tawney had other things to say about the working class, of a more challenging and troublesome kind, but at the centre of his thought remained the vision of the commonality of a class becoming the attribute of a nation.

The vision of a nation united around common ends could be glimpsed, if only fleetingly, in other directions too. It is impossible to read Tawney's commentary on the Great War, or even the Second World War, without being struck by his powerful sense of the moral unity of the event and of the need to extend such unity from the organisation for war to the social organisation of peace. In 1916 he could write of the 'fellowship in a moral idea or purpose' which sustained an army in the trenches; and in 1940 he could tell the American public that the British people were united around the conviction that they were 'defending certain simple moralities'.[15] In other words, wars were about ends, or should be, and were an example of the unity of effort and cohesiveness of purpose which such moral agreement brought with it. Both to be true to the war, and to learn the lesson of this example, it was necessary to carry the moral unity of war through into the task of social reconstruction and into the durable fabric of social life. In this sense, then, war taught an important lesson and, in its social impact, opened up the opportunity of acting upon it.

Tawney's concern with a unity of common ends, and the influence of this on his thought, may be further illustrated in a different area. As was seen earlier, his advocacy of 'freedom' in industry and the diffusion of power in society stopped short at the point beyond which a community of common purpose might be threatened. It was this which distanced him from one strand of guild socialism and prevented (unlike both Cole and Laski) any flirtation with pluralism. His stern message to industrial workers was that 'if they are to exercise corporate freedom, they must be ready to undertake corporate responsibility'.[16] What was needed was a functional freedom for public service not a sectional freedom for private interest:

> Any reorganisation of industry must not merely satisfy the demand for industrial freedom; it must also supply the machinery through which the public may secure efficient service. Industry, after all, is a social function, and its reform must not merely promise a higher status to privileged groups, but must carry with it an assurance of the subordination of individual and corporate interests to those of the community.[17]

If freedom as power was part of Tawney's message, then freedom as subordination was another part. The aim was to organise society for a common purpose, not to buttress group autonomy. The objective was social unity and integration on the basis of common ends, not fragmentation and sectionalism on the basis of private ends.

If all this emphasises the centrality of this theme across the range of Tawney's work, it also indicates some of the difficulties associated with it. The suggestion, framed most directly in his

87

pre-1914 diary, that a social consensus on 'ends' should be established which had the effect of confining political conflict and
disagreement to the level of 'means', was surely a fantasy, and
in some hands a dangerous fantasy. It is tempting to say that it
could only have been made in the world before 1914, before the
period in which ideologies and political movements acted upon
it, except for the fact that a British Conservative Prime Minister
in 1986 could announce as her fundamental aim the elimination
of socialist ideas and their carriers from the political agenda, so
that there might be agreement about the ends of politics and
political competition only about the means of achieving them.
This mode of thought, whether from Tawney or Thatcher, is
fundamentally unpolitical, not because there is any suggestion
that ends are to be imposed by coercion or from above, nor
because there is anything improper about the desire to win a
position of ideological hegemony for a particular view of the
world, but because it is part of the essence of a politically free
society that there should be abundant opportunities to explore
both the ends and means of political life with tolerant vigour.
This was not true of the medieval world, nor of inter-war China,
whatever their other achievements. The desire for a morally
rooted social unity is admirable, but not if it evades problems of
ethical diversity, social pluralism and political freedom. To the
extent that Tawney's position did evade such difficulties, a
philosophy of common ends comes perilously close to being a
philosophy of loose ends.

Nor is it the case that political ends and means can *in fact* be
so neatly separated, as Tawney, in other moods, was the first to
recognise. The world of 'means' is a realm of values too, especially
of a procedural kind, and political life presents problems of means
and ends at the same time. It makes more sense, therefore, to
read Tawney's espousal of a society of common ends as an argument about the progress to be made towards, and the benefits

to be gained from, a set of shared values of the right kind. Moreover, this enterprise has to be seen less in terms of the apocalyptic spirit of wartime and more in terms of the humdrum realities of everyday social life. In his pre-1914 diary, Tawney had reflected, and wanted others to reflect, on the 'golden moments in the life of mankind when national aims seem to be bent for some noble purpose, and men live at peace in the harmony which springs from the possession of a common moral ideal'.[18] Yet it is doubtful whether 'golden moments' of social harmony and moral unity provide a reliable basis upon which to approach the durable task of remoralising a society in which these are merely interludes from business as usual. Certainly this was Tawney's own gloomy verdict on the collapse of moral unity during and after the Great War. It is confirmed by the periodically pathetic invocations of the 'Dunkirk spirit' by politicians who, lost at sea in the present, seek to live off the moral capital of a golden moment at sea in the past.

Turning from the matter of common ends to the argument about the moral imperative of treating people as ends and not as means, Tawney's position may be further elucidated. It was noticed earlier, but needs to be emphasised here, that Tawney presented this as the fundamental moral axiom, the key to everything else, but he presented it not as a moral argument but as a moral truth. Either it was believed or it was not; if it was not believed, then that was that; but if it was believed, then it carried with it certain inescapable implications for the way in which society was arranged which, if not acted upon, was both a moral hypocrisy and the cause of serious social and economic difficulties. Hence his familiar maxim that: 'One cannot argue with the choice of a soul; and, if men like that kind of dog, then that is the kind of dog they like'.[19] Differences about ends were beyond the reach of argument, for 'such differences lie too deep to be settled by argument, whether they appear in the sixteenth century or in our own day'.[20] It is clear, then, that Tawney's appeal was to a moral sensibility, which needed to be aroused and cultivated, not to a philosophical sensibility requiring argument and explanation. He confessed happily to believing that 'truths concealed from the wise and learned are apt to be revealed to babes' and that 'as far as the principles, though not the techniques for applying them, are concerned, I put my money on the latter'.[21]

This was, perhaps, an unsatisfactory and insecure basis upon which to construct a general argument, in so far as it rested upon a take-it-or-leave-it moral premise which was pronounced as unarguable with. There is, after all, a philosophical pedigree to an argument about treating people as ends and not as means. There is, further, something a little paradoxical about the construction of an essentially *moral* case for socialism on a foundation of values which is unexplored and, it is said, unexplorable by moral argument. However, that was Tawney's position, accurately reflecting its source in his Christian faith (even if sometimes also invoking the support of the moral sensibility of a general tradition of Western humanism). What he was concerned to do, and where he comes into his own as a social thinker, was to press the implications for social organisation of holding this moral position. This was, as has already been seen, a major theme of his work.

Yet the character of Tawney's project, on the matter of treating people as ends, had other aspects too. If moral arousal was the task, then it was necessary to jolt an awareness of the values, the view of ends, contained within social institutions, practices and pronouncements. His question, as he inspects the social world, is always: what scale of values, what view of human beings, is reflected here? Because 'social institutions are the visible expression of the scale of moral values which rules the minds of individuals',[22] individuals had to be confronted with the moral basis of these institutions and challenged by the extent of their departure from a proper valuation of human beings as ends. Thus Tawney is constantly stripping off the social and ideological veneer to reveal the view of ends concealed beneath. One striking example of this procedure in action is provided by his dissection of a memorandum from the Federation of British Industries opposing the provisions of the 1918 Education Act on the grounds that an extension of education would damage industry. Behind this unsustainable argument, Tawney finds ('in a charming sentence, which reveals in a flash the view which it takes both of the function of the working classes in society and the meaning of education') a repulsive morality, in which an excess of education is regarded as 'unsuitable' for an entire class of children: 'There it is, the whole Master Class theory of society in a sentence!'[23] This belief, that there are classes who are ends and classes who are means, could not be disproved ('any more than one can disprove a taste for militarism, or for drugs, or for bad novels'), but what could be done was to 'expose its consequences' for the organisation of society.

This example highlights Tawney's method and approach. Facts could be disputed and the arguments based upon them refuted (like the argument that increased educational provision was economically damaging), but matters of 'ultimate belief' were beyond argument, for 'those who think that men are first of all men have no premise in common with those who think, like the authors of the Federation's Memorandum, that they are first of all servants, or animals, or tools'. However, it was important to identify the belief which sustained particular positions and to reveal its range of consequences. Much of Tawney's work is concerned with this dual task of illuminating lines of connection, backwards from social institutions and policies to their underlying values, forwards from values which are held to the social consequences of holding them. Moreover, this process of illumination performed an important service of public persuasion, for beliefs such as those which sustained the educational policies of the Federation of British Industries had 'only to be stated, in order to be rejected decisively by the public opinion of the community'. If beliefs could not be argued with, they could and should be shown for what they were, thereby challenging moral sensibilities and so influencing opinion and policy. Often it was a small detail – an incident, a statement, an instance – which, if examined (as Tawney frequently did) threw a flood of light on the values at issue.

Tawney's exercises in value-stripping were one expression of his emphasis on the question of whether human beings were regarded as ends or as means. However, if his purpose in this was moral arousal rather than moral argument, this was not the case when he approached the question from another direction. When he spoke as a Christian to other Christians both his tone and message were sharply different. The essential difference was that he was now addressing people who already shared his Christian belief in the equal valuation of human beings, as ends and not as means, as the individual children of the universal family of God. However, while sharing this moral premise with Tawney, many of his co-religionists managed to avoid sharing his conclusions about its implications for the arrangement of social and economic life. It was with such people, and their churches, that Tawney always maintained a particular argument, of an uncompromising kind. Worse even than those people who were deaf to a moral appeal were those who claimed to believe in certain values but refused their application to social life. This was not moral deafness but moral hypocrisy.

Tawney's charge, then, was that the Christian churches combined a doctrine about the importance of treating people as ends with an acquiescence in a social and economic system which treated them unequally and instrumentally as means. His *Religion and the Rise of Capitalism* was designed, in considerable measure, to frame this charge in historical terms. More generally, his argument had two related aspects, both concerned with the implications of the moral premise of Christianity. First, it was necessary to accept, contrary to prevailing practice, that there was a unity of personal and social life and thus no justification for confining Christian principles to the realm of private conduct and denying their extension to the conduct of social and economic affairs. Such a 'convenient dualism' was false both to the nature of man and of Christianity:

> Life might be simpler if it were possible to serve one master in the privacy of one's chamber and another in the market-place and assembly; but the world does not seem to be made that way. Man is an amphibious animal. He belongs to two worlds, and leads in both of them, not successively but simultaneously, a life which is one.[24]

This line of argument was intended to persuade Christians that they could not avoid having a social philosophy. However, it was supplemented by a second line of argument suggesting that they could equally not avoid having a social philosophy of a particular kind. Here Tawney's unequivocal proposition was that capitalism was 'not so much un-Christian as anti-Christian',[25] for the essential capitalist virtues were the essential Christian vices and produced consequences which were 'an odious outrage on the image of God' and the tolerance of which was an 'essay in blasphemy'. Tawney was never more ferocious, or his irony more savage, than when contemplating the 'humiliating exhibition' of the leaders of Christian thought who mouthed moral platitudes while refusing to point their social application: 'Such evasions disgust sincere men, and bring Christianity into contempt'. If the choice of a soul was beyond argument, those who had chosen a soul but failed to pursue the implications of their choice deserved to have the Book thrown at them.

93

Then there is the next sense in which Tawney wanted to talk about means and ends. This involved the assertion that what primarily mattered about an institution, a movement or a doctrine was the end towards which its face was set, and that this defining characteristic should be kept firmly in view when the secondary issues of means and machinery were discussed. Tawney emerges as someone who combined a rigidity about ends with a flexibility about means, and this provides at least part of the reason why he has won admirers from such diverse ideological quarters. He was an extremist about ends who could also be a moderate about means. Expediency, to employ one of his familiar terms, was entirely appropriate at the level of means, but thoroughly inappropriate when ends were at issue. It is necessary to look briefly at how this general approach was reflected in his work, and at some of its difficulties.

The fact that ends were paramount did not lead Tawney to conclude that the means by which progress towards them might be made were of little interest or significance. If means should not be confused with ends, and their secondary character not forgotten, standing as they did in the status of technique in relation to values, they nevertheless mattered considerably. When Tawney discussed China he emphasised the centrality of a unified conception of ends in Chinese life, but this did not prevent him stressing the need for China to develop the means whereby the organisation of reform could be undertaken: 'The first problem, which lies behind all questions of particular reforms, is vast and fundamental. It is not who shall govern the State, but whether there shall be a State at all. It is whether public power shall exist'.[26] A conception of ends was important, more important ultimately than anything else, but it was also not enough.

When Tawney discussed such matters nearer home, he was no less attentive to questions of means, even while ensuring that the discussion never lost sight of the fundamental values and ends involved. What distinguished his approach to almost every question he touched was the need to get the principles right first, for it was here that the real difficulties occurred, and upon this secure basis to adopt a flexible stance in relation to methods of implementation and machinery. In this way it was possible, and desirable, to combine a dogmatism about ends with a pragmatism about means. Tawney did not claim that the discovery of effective techniques was always easy, but he did insist that it was never sufficiently difficult and unyielding to justify a failure to act upon principles. If there was a will, then several ways could certainly be found. Similarly, it was always possible to ensure by appropriate techniques that the organisational dangers allegedly involved in the implementation of certain principles were mitigated or removed.

This approach informs the whole of Tawney's work and has been noticed at several points in earlier chapters. Arguments about machinery should not be confused with arguments about principles and should be conducted in a flexible and malleable spirit. The broad direction was important, not the precise organisational details, and there was ample scope for diversity and experimentation. Thus the principle of functional property was consistent with a variety of forms of property ownership. Nationalisation was a method not a principle, appropriate in some areas but not appropriate in others, and to be seen as part of a large family of socialisation techniques. The organisation of industry was amenable to a variety of structural forms. The principle of equality was consistent with considerable diversity of treatment and with differential rewards. It was quite possible to have public ownership without bureaucracy if this was planned for: 'The idea that public ownership *necessarily* involves red tape, centralisation, officialdom, is, in fact, an illusion. It *may* suffer from these vices, if it is organised so as to encourage them. . . It *need* not do so, if care is taken to avoid them'.[27] The socialist should approach organisational matters flexibly and experimentally, with public ownership in particular regarded as a 'laboratory' for different structures and techniques. The organisation of socialism should be thought of 'not in terms of a single bottle-neck through which socialist re-organisation must be forced' but in terms of 'a multitude of growing points'.[28]

On every front, then, Tawney's approach to the question of means was of this character. If he forced the question of ends back to fundamentals, he eschewed such fundamentalism in relation to means. In the realm of expediency everything was provisional and conditional. If ends were agreed, then means could always be found. Thus if the idea of equality was accepted, the 'technique' of acting upon it comprised measures which were 'the most familiar of commonplaces'.[29] If the principle of function was accepted, then its practical application in terms of property ownership presented no great difficulties. There were no overwhelming problems involved in combining public direction of the economy with markets and consumer freedom. And so on. Did Tawney merely succeed in making the 'means' of socialism sound easier than it was, or was ever likely to be?

There are grounds for thinking that he did, even in terms of his own range of examples. Leave aside his failure to say anything substantial about how a socialist economy might actually operate, on which he offered reassurance (mainly in response to the warnings from his colleague, Hayek) but little else. This was not a matter on which Tawney claimed any expertise, and his silence was echoed by a whole tradition. Consider rather the matters on which he did have substantial things to say. One example is his argument for public ownership as a derivation from the principle of function applied to property. This is the argument deployed in *The Acquisitive Society* and forms the basis of his case for the conversion of the ownership of the bulk of industry from private to public hands in order to eliminate functionless shareholding. However, a generation later, the principle has become that of subjecting the economic system to 'public control', whether through ownership or 'regulation', for these are merely 'species of one genus'.[30] The principle has clearly changed, the method been modified, and the programmatic consequences made more indeterminate. This suggests a rather more elusive and difficult relationship between the ends and means of socialism, even in this key terrain, than the form of his argument usually implied, a difficulty exacerbated rather than dispelled by his consistently generous proclivity for embracing as 'species of one genus' policies which others frequently viewed as discordant. This may explain why it was sometimes easier to see Tawney's principles than to be clear where, exactly, they led; and why those who shared his ends could nevertheless disagree so fundamentally about what was implied by them in terms of means.

There are further examples, even more central to his distinctive preoccupations, where similar difficulties may be detected. He had a particular concern with education, using it as a litmus test of general social values, and demanding its reconstruction in the name of equal worth and a common culture. He argued, elegantly and effectively, that liberty and equality were not antithetical values but mutually nourishing. He insisted that equality of treatment was not identity of treatment, and that the principle was perfectly consistent with diversity and variety. In all these respects Tawney was the schoolmaster to a generation of British socialists. But where exactly did Tawney's instruction lead? He argued, as was noticed earlier, that equality and a common culture demanded that all children should attend the same schools and that it was the peculiar and vicious vice of the English class system in education that they did not. So did this mean the abolition of the public schools? Did it mean that nothing less than the comprehensive principle (or 'multilateral' as it was earlier called) would be acceptable?

When Tawney is consulted on these questions, the answers turn out to be much less straightforward. He has no difficulty in describing private education as doing 'more than any other single cause, except capitalism itself, to perpetuate the division of the nation into classes',[31] but all he can propose as a remedy is that private schools should be 'required. . . to hold a licence from the Board of Education' specifying certain conditions about access. Similarly, despite his espousal of the link between common schooling and common culture, he was in practice unfriendly towards the concept of a multilateral school (except experimentally) and emphasised the need to encourage 'vertical mobility' by matching 'capacity' with 'the type of education best fitted to develop it'.[32] His welcome for the 1944 Education Act, with its selective basis, reflected this outlook: 'There is no reason to suppose that the modern secondary schools will necessarily be regarded as inferior to the more specialised grammar and technical secondary schools. On the contrary, the former, if wisely planned, are likely to provide the education best calculated to give the majority of boys and girls a hopeful start in life'.[33] Thus it has been possible to claim a major role for Tawney in propagating a position which has 'proved to be the Achilles heel of Labour's post-war educational policy'.[34]

However, the point here is not to discuss whether Tawney was right or wrong, but to suggest that even in terms of his own examples the relationship between ends and means was more problematical than his general approach allowed for. Agreement about ends did not preclude fundamental disagreement about means, nor did it necessarily act as a solvent of the real difficulties of machinery and implementation (even if these were approached in a spirit of pragmatic diversity). Partly, this was because Tawney's 'ends', as is usually the case, consisted not of a single value, uncompromised and uncompromising, but of a cluster of values; and the problem of 'means' had therefore to reflect this cluster and effect some compromise and accommodation between them. The point is not that such values are inconsistent, but that they are plural. Partly, too, the difficulties derived from the fact that the world of practice, not least of socialist practice, has shown itself to be rather more intractable than Tawney's approach often seemed to suggest. What he was prone to describe as 'mere questions of machinery'[35] have proved more problematical for socialists, even for those with a secure conception of socialist ends, than might have been anticipated from such a description of their secondary and instrumental status.

Turning now, briefly, to that further sense in which Tawney spoke of ends, as a reference point of valuation against which policies, movements and doctrines were to be judged, this provided a practical test (albeit of a spiritual kind) which ensured that bad means could not defend themselves by a doctrine of good ends. At every stage, in every place, Tawney wanted to know what the effect of policies and doctrines was on the lives of individual human beings, in a qualitative not quantitative sense, *qua* human beings, in terms of opportunities for freedom and self-develoment. This we may call the Dubb Test, in honour of the ubiquitous Henry Dubb ('the civilian equivalent of the P.B.I. or poor bloody infantry, i.e. the common, courageous, good-hearted, patient, proletarian fool')[36] who was never far from Tawney's elbow, especially in the 1930s. If capitalism failed this test (and fascism even more so, of course), then so too did a certain kind of Christianity and a certain kind of socialism:

> A Christianity which resigns the economic world to the devil appears to me, in short, not Christianity at all; Capitalism a juggernaut sacrificing human ends to the idolatry of material means; and a Socialism which puts Dubb on a chain and prevents him from teaching manners to his exalted governors a Socialism – if such it can be called – which has more than half its battles still before it.[37]

Tawney's own position was clearly stated: 'In the interminable case of *Dubb v. Superior Persons and Co.,* whether Christians, Capitalists or Communists, I am an unrepentant Dubbite'.[38]

It was as an 'unrepentant Dubbite' that Tawney kept his democratic socialist head in the 1930s when many others on the Left were eagerly losing theirs. Watching the world divide itself into 'credal blocks', he hung on to Henry Dubb and wondered if the real division of the future would lie 'less between different forms of political and economic organisation than between different estimates of the value to be put on the muddled soul of Henry Dubb'.[39] For Tawney, it should be recorded, there was no totalitarian temptation. 'Tawney's contempt for our ruling class is more intense than ours', Beatrice Webb observed, 'but he does not share our faith in Soviet Communism'.[40] If the Dubb Test provided a safe path through the ideological turbulence of the 1930s, it also offered a yardstick by which to assess the social and economic reforms of the 1940s. In this case, though, the test was passed, for these measures would enable the individual to 'enjoy a better prospect of growing to his full stature, and of turning his mature capacities to good account'.[41] The content of the measures might be quantitative, but their impact and evaluation was qualitative, extending the powers of Henry Dubb and improving his access to the means of civilisation.

However, Tawney also employed the Dubb Test in a further sense, which brings the discussion, finally, to the question of ends and means as political method or strategy, on which Tawney had much to say. His focus was on Western social democracy (for 'dams, bridges, power-plants and steel-works, however admirable, are not a substitute for human rights; and the contrast between Russian Police Collectivism and the socialism of Western Europe is too obvious to need emphasis')[42] but his particular focus was on the character and strategy of socialism in Britain. Sometimes his remarks are *about* British socialism, explaining and defending it to the outside world; at other times, they are directed *to* British socialists, often in a sharply critical vein. To the former audience, British socialism is presented as essentially ethical in its inspiration and ends, having democracy at its centre not merely as an instrument but as a value, and engaged in the task of extending democracy and freedom from the political realm to the social and economic. To the latter audience, the message is that this is what British socialism *should* be about. The important point is that Tawney had a strong sense of the appropriate strategy for socialism in Britain, and pressed it with vigour.

He pressed it with particular vigour in the 1930s, when, first, the Labour Party needed to be reminded that its purpose was socialism and, later, when some socialists needed to be reminded that their method was democracy. The first reminder was delivered in Tawney's celebrated post-mortem on the ignominious life and death of the second Labour Government (1929-31), published in 1932 as 'The Choice Before the Labour Party', but properly regarded as his general verdict on the political strategy of British socialism. Labour's failure in office was the failure of a whole tradition. Lacking a 'creed', in the form of 'a common conception of the ends of political action, and of the means of achieving them, based on a common view of the life proper to human beings, and of the steps required at any moment more nearly to attain it',[43] Labour suffered from a disability which, if not remedied, would eventually prove fatal. It was organised around an internal vacuum. Hence its collapse into conventionality and futility, symbolised by its participation in the sordid business of political honours and titles. The only antidote was a resolute commitment to socialism, and an equally resolute political strategy in pursuit of this end. Thus Labour should give priority to socialism, not the satisfaction of sectional interests. It should concentrate its efforts on the essential task of winning economic power, not on offering 'the largest number of carrots to the largest possible number of donkeys'. It should explain frankly how arduous its project was, not how easy. It should aim to make socialists, not merely to win voters. Above all, Labour in office should be 'audacious', knowing that there were limits to what it could do but pressing right up against them. If Labour did not become a party of this kind, then its future was necessarily one of degeneration and disillusionment; and it was better that capitalism should be run by capitalists, who at least believed in it even if they had difficulty in making it work.

If this was the first part of Tawney's tract on socialist method and strategy, it was soon supplemented by a second part. The major source here is a new chapter on 'Democracy and Socialism' which Tawney added to *Equality* in 1938. The context is no longer merely the futility of Labour in office, but the ideological alarums and excursions on the Left in the decade following. Tawney retracts nothing from his earlier remarks, insisting on a political boldness which 'means a decisive break with the whole policy of capitalist governments, or it means nothing at all',[44] but now adds a lecture on the need for socialists to be 'both sensible and trenchant'. The trouble with British socialists was that they 'frequently conduct themselves as though the most certain method of persuading the public to feel complete confidence in their cause were to convince it that they feel no confidence in each other'. The sectarianism of 'private socialisms' had become rife, and 'invitations to hunt tigers were issued by sportsmen with whom a brave man might well hesitate to shoot rabbits'. Tawney, like Orwell, reserved a particular anger for the dialectical diversions practised by socialist intellectuals in the 1930s who (as he said in a speech at this time) 'use language which really has no meaning unless some form of violent revolution is what it means, and thus, since in fact they mean nothing of the kind, they are condemned to sterility'.[45] They needed to be reminded that, as far as the alleged differences between a left and right wing were concerned, 'nine-tenths of them are nonsense' since there was a fundamental unity of ends; and that a politics organised around such differences simply produced an impression of 'wearisome futility' on people like Henry Dubb. The point was not that socialists should eschew 'extreme' opinions but that 'they should show extreme sense in reaching them, extreme self-restraint in keeping their mouths shut till the opinions are worth stating, and extreme resolution in acting on them, when stated'.

These remarks introduced the further sense in which Tawney invoked the Dubb Test. Socialism had to make its appeal not to mankind in general but to the 'political psychology' of people in a particular time and place. In Britain, this meant an appeal to minds 'steeped for two centuries in a liberal tradition', not least to a working class mind which was most attached of all to the 'elementary decencies' associated with this tradition. The lesson for socialists was clear:

> They must face the fact that, if the public, and particularly the working-class public, is confronted with the choice between capitalist democracy, with all its nauseous insincerities, and unde-mocratic socialism, it will choose the former every time. They must make it clear beyond the possibility of doubt that the socialist commonwealth which they preach will be built on democratic foun-dations. That fact is a proof, not of stupidity, but of intelligence. It means that Henry Dubb has the sense to prefer two good things to one. . . In becoming a socialist, he has no intention of surrendering his rights as a citizen, which, after all, he once fought pretty hard to win'.

This lesson in British political culture, and in the political psycho-logy of Henry Dubb, was one which Tawney pressed on British socialists as an elementary political truth. It was true in two senses, because only a democratic socialism was worth having but, also, because only a political strategy based upon it stood any chance of success. A failure to learn this lesson imposed an unnecessary disability upon a socialism which was 'no longer bad politics in England, unless socialists choose to make it so, which some of them do with a quite surprising ingenuity'.

So here was Tawney the party man, firmly attached to the Labour Party as the political vehicle of socialism in Britain, but who also offered one of the most powerful accounts of the assorted infirmities which characterised Labour-Socialism and prevented it from performing the role assigned to it. This has led at least one critic to argue that Tawney was 'curiously blind to how greatly his declared ends and his chosen means were at odds with one another'.[46] Did Labour-Socialism really have a set of common ends, so that there could be no disagreement over essentials? Certainly this belief always informed Tawney's own political stance, which explains why someone whose conception of socialist ends placed him firmly on the left could nevertheless be found lining up with the right (as with his support for the pro-Gaitskell Campaign for Democratic Socialism in 1960-61 to 'resist the leftward trend in the Party',[47] despite the evident incompatibility between his own view of socialism and that of these 'revisionists'). As Labour argued about defence policy, Tawney (who was strongly anti-unilateralist and anti-neutralist) wanted to point out that there was frequently no such thing as a socialist defence policy.[48] The question which Tawney did not consider was whether the real problem was that Labour was a coalition of uncommon ends, as well as of uncertain means. Nor did he question whether the rest of the political machinery in Britain was quite so amenable to socialist purposes as he seemed to assume; or whether the state was really just the 'serviceable drudge'[49] that he proclaimed it to be. However, the reason why he was not detained by such questions was not an oversight, but an authentic expression of the standpoint discussed in the next chapter.

5 Choosing equality

'What matters to the health of society is the objective towards which its face is set'.

To understand Tawney it is necessary to understand what he meant when, echoing Matthew Arnold, he urged his society to 'choose equality'. This is not quite as straightforward as it sounds. What is at issue here is not the choice of equality, but equality as choice. In other words, it is the extent to which Tawney made the activity of moral choice central to his formulation of the socialist project. Further, it is the extent to which he made values and ideas central to his account of the historical process of which this project was a part. In both respects, the extent was considerable, and takes us to the heart of Tawney's socialism of moral choice. This may be seen as the source of his characteristic strengths, or of his characteristic weaknesses, but it is undeniably the site where the distinctive quality of his socialist thought has to be explored.

This site can be identified a little more clearly if it is remembered that Tawney was both a prescriptive social thinker and an economic historian. As the former, he wanted to promote certain social values, on the grounds both of their intrinsic merit as values and the social benefits to be obtained from their adoption. As the latter, he wanted to examine 'the struggle of ideas and interests'[1] in the past, and to make connections with similar struggles in the present. His concern to establish such connections also established the unity of his thought (to the chagrin of some of his professional colleagues). However, there are questions about the nature of these connections. If a politics of moral choice was prescribed in the present, how did this relate to the analysis of social change in the past? Did the attention given to the struggle of ideas in the present reflect a verdict on the historical balance of the struggle of ideas and interests? What exactly was the relationship between ideas and interests in the historical process? Tawney was not the kind of thinker to give extended, theoretical treatment to such questions, but it is possible to identify his general approach to them. In doing so, the question to be kept in mind is this: Was Tawney the social moralist recommending that society *ought* to be reconstructed through the political choice of values, or was Tawney the economic historian suggesting that societies *were* reconstructed by this means?

Tawney was certainly an 'idealist', in the sense that he attributed a particular importance to ideas and values. As a social thinker he made these central to his analysis of the social problem and of its solution, while as an historian he gave special attention to the role of 'opinion' during the periods he studied. Indeed, it is possible to present his thought as representing an idealism of a rather extreme kind. In his pre-1914 diary, as was seen earlier, he rejected any materialist interpretation of the prevailing labour unrest in favour of an interpretation which emphasised the effect of the propagation of ideas and values; while, more generally, he insisted that the *only* route to durable social change lay through a change in 'the ideas which control men in their ordinary actions'. Other 'mechanical' routes, whether of the kind favoured by Marxists or Fabians, were a chimera. The argument of *The Acquisitive Society* was organised around the proposition that 'an appeal to principles is the condition of any considerable reconstruction of society' and, because social institutions were reflections of the moral values of individuals, the further proposition that 'it is impossible to alter institutions without altering that valuation'. The reason for this was simple: 'Parliament, industrial organisations, the whole complex machinery through which society expresses itself, is a mill which grinds only what is put into it'.[2]

For a thinker who, elsewhere, displayed an acute sense of the extent to which the economic system was a system of power, this formulation may be thought to exhibit an idealism which is both excessive and eccentric. It was not necessary to be a Marxist to doubt whether social change required a movement of principles, or whether social institutions were really the expression of individual values, or whether such institutions were unalterable without an alteration in the moral values of individuals. Was Tawney seriously suggesting that the 'machinery' of society could not be sustained by the exercise of power, only of values, and that this power could not be rooted in a group sectionalism whether of class or another kind, only in individuals, and social reconstruction could be effected only from below, not from above? Further, instead of deriving social institutions from the ideas and values of individuals, did it not make at least as much sense (and often more) to derive such ideas and values from the ideological influence exerted by dominant social institutions?

Faced with these questions, it is perhaps more sensible to regard Tawney as engaged in a politics of moral exhortation rather than of social explanation. The aim was to persuade people how much could be accomplished by a movement of individual moral values, and how little could be accomplished without this. In order to effect social change it was necessary to embrace certain moral ideas and to have the will to act upon them. Moral sensibility and growth were operationalised by an energy of will. Certainly Tawney was always anxious to emphasise how much could be achieved if people only wanted and willed it enough. Capitalism and its false philosophy could be swept away when enough people wanted to do so. Far from being indomitable, the present economic system was essentially fragile. Thus he explained how the functionless character of property in modern capitalism represented an 'atrophy' which presaged demise: 'The hold which a class has upon the future depends on the function which it performs. What nature demands is work; few working aristocracies, however tyrannical, have fallen; few functionless aristocracies have survived. In society, as in the world of organic life, atrophy is but one stage removed from death'.[3] This could scarcely be regarded, and was perhaps not intended, as a serious rule of historical sociology, as though the power of capitalism to maintain and reproduce itself counted for little compared with the fact that, functionally speaking, it was increasingly against 'nature'. What it could be regarded as was an attempt to strengthen the historical resolve of the functional class to supplant the functionless.

There are many other instances of the way in which Tawney not merely advocated a politics of moral choice but insisted on its effectiveness if pursued with sufficient will and vigour. In other words, choosing equality was not merely a moral choice but also a viable political strategy (and, at bottom, the only durably viable strategy). Discussing the nature of power, and the changing basis of social power at different historical periods, he combines an emphasis on its importance for social analysis with a conclusion that:

> Men exercise only the power that they are allowed to exercise by other men. . . Its ultimate seat is – to use an unfashionable word – the soul. . . It is thus both awful and fragile, and can dominate a continent, only in the end to be blown down by a whisper. To destroy it, nothing more is required than to be indifferent to its threats, and to prefer other goods to those which it promises. Nothing less, however, is required also.[4]

No sooner is power conjured up than it is put down. He frequently tells socialists that the obstacles in their path are really just 'ghosts' and 'shadows' and that 'those who have the impertinence to walk up to ghosts can usually walk through them'.[5]

The issues raised by such remarks are fundamental to Tawney's whole position as a socialist thinker. How could people develop the impertinence to walk through ghosts? This, in one form or another, is the quintessential Tawney question. For him, therefore, the real terrain of struggle is that to which he applied such terms as 'temper', 'spirit' and 'habit of mind'. This, of course, is precisely the terrain to which, from first to last, he addressed his own attention and energy. The socialist objective, to borrow a famous formulation from Marx, was not merely that of emancipation but of self-emancipation. 'However the socialist ideal may be expressed', Tawney once remarked, 'few things could be more remote from it than a herd of tame animals with wise rulers in command'.[6] It was Orwell who distinguished between a socialism in which the working class acts and one in which it is acted upon, and this was also Tawney's distinction. It differentiated his conception of democratic socialism from the various forms of authoritarian collectivism, whether cast in a Marxist or Fabian mould. He recalled late in life how Beatrice Webb ('one whom I revere') nevertheless 'once froze my blood, by remarking that she desired to establish "a regimen of mental and moral hygiene" for her long-suffering fellow countrymen'.[7] Democratic socialism, by contrast, wanted to release human energies for an active citizenship of common ends.

But how? Tawney's answer concentrated on the cultivation and stimulation of the human 'temper'. Inequality would be ended when the habit of mind which sustained it, the 'religion of inequality', no longer held sway. Freedom would be achieved when people were no longer prepared to be treated as means instead of ends. Tawney's own work, in both the manner of its construction and the character of its argument, was designed to make an impact on a habit of mind which was held to be the key to

109

everything else. He clearly also regarded education as having a significant role to play in this enterprise. If the workers' education movement was important as an arena of active citizenship, a training ground and an example, the general extension of educational provision was also important if citizens were to be developed who would be satisfied with nothing less than freedom and would have the confidence to pursue it. The elementary schools had at least done something to 'straighten the backs of the mass of the population',[8] and a decent secondary education could be expected to do more in this direction.

It is interesting that his discussion of welfare provision reflects this same consideration. Not only was the extension of welfare services valuable in itself, but it was also valuable because of its effects on the character and temper of those affected by it. Thus it was 'clap-trap' to dismiss the social services as mere palliatives, for they produced a growth in human vigour which 'dissolves the servile complex' and so contributed to 'the creation of a population with the nerve and self-confidence to face without shrinking the immense task of socialist reconstruction'.[9] Further, Tawney wanted to suggest that there was a dynamic process at work whereby social expenditure, in its impact on the outlook of individuals, changed social psychology and 'the altered psychology acts as a permanent force modifying social structure, which in turn, as it is transformed, sets minds and wills at work to insist on further modifications'.[10] Here, as elsewhere, much has to be taken on trust from Tawney, who had a persuasive tendency to dress propositions up as axioms. Why should welfare necessarily strengthen a culture of independence and self-confidence rather than one of dependency and subordination? Why should welfare act as a stimulant to equality, rather than as a substitute for it? Perhaps all that can really be said is that Tawney's socialism of 'minds and wills' required that it should.

However, it would be wrong to give the impression that

Tawney's socialism depended upon a belief in steady moral growth or effortless exertions of will. If he recommended a socialism of moral choice it was not because it was easy but because, though difficult, it was the only means whereby a genuinely transformed social order could be achieved and sustained. If he emphasised the ability of mind and will to change the world, he also emphasised the scale of the task. His material was individual human beings, yet he viewed this material not through the benign lens of a perfectionist theory of human nature but through the harsh light of a doctrine of original sin. In this sense, Tawney's socialism was neither 'scientific' nor 'utopian'. When he pressed the need to subordinate economic activities to a social purpose, he acknowledged that this was 'not easy' because it required 'a constant effort of will, against which egotistical instincts are in rebellion'.[11] There is no trace in his thought of a 'natural' goodness thwarted only by its environment, or of a plastic human nature waiting only to be moulded to an appropriate shape by social technicians. Instead, there is the conviction that 'the heart of man holds mysteries of contradiction which live in vigorous incompatibility together' and that 'in every human soul there is a socialist and an individualist, an authoritarian and a fanatic for liberty, as in each there is a Catholic and a Protestant'.[12] Social institutions were important in fostering one type of character rather than another, but no institutional arrangement was proof against the contradictions of human nature. Tawney's socialist project had individual human beings as its material, but human beings as they were.

Similarly, he refused to attribute simplicities of character to a social class when he had denied them to individuals. Tawney was an intellectual who put himself at the service of the working class movement (and with an active conception of this role which made him politically effective),[13] but he was not one of that breed of socialist intellectuals which bestowed upon the working class either a special humanity or a historical destiny. He was less concerned to argue that the working class was the carrier of socialism than to suggest that it was all too easy for it to settle for something else. 'The workers cannot have it both ways', announced *The Acquisitive Society:* 'They must choose whether to assume the responsibility for industrial discipline and become free, or to repudiate it and continue to be serfs'.[14] Several pages of *Equality* are devoted to the problem that the workers are 'too willing to accept the moral premises of their masters', as evidenced by their preoccupation with wages and neglect of fundamental issues, an indifference to inequality, a tolerance of subordination, and 'in their hearts' a desire to be capitalists themselves if they could be. When the working-class movement fell 'below itself' in this way, what it came to desire was 'not a social order of a different kind, in which money and economic power will no longer be the criterion of achievement, but a social order of the same kind, in which money and economic power will be somewhat differently distributed'.[15] Reviewing the condition of British socialism in the early 1950s, and noting the failure of the post-war Labour Government to bring about a change in the economic status of workers, Tawney believed ('to speak frankly') that the obstacle to change was provided not only by employers: 'It is the apathy and torpor of many workers, who in theory desire freedom, but who in practice are too often reluctant to assume the burdens without which freedom cannot be had'.[16]

Choosing equality, then, was a difficult enterprise, both for individuals and for classes. However, it was difficult less because of the opposition to be overcome or the problems of policy and machinery to be tackled, than because of the lack of 'a strong root of independent conviction to nourish and sustain it'.[17] This does not mean that Tawney was dismissive about the opposition, or uninterested in the machinery. Indeed, he more than once reminded the Labour movement that it was up against 'the oldest and toughest plutocracy in the world', which consisted of 'agreeable, astute, forcible, self-confident, and, when hard-pressed, unscrupulous people, who know pretty well which side their bread is buttered, and intend that the supply of butter shall not run short'.[18] However, the lesson from this was not that it was unchallengeable, or that only a revolutionary challenge was possible, but that it would not succumb to anything less than a sustained effort of mind and will. Tawney gave the same answer to those who identified problems of structure and machinery as the essential problems, even when that structure was the state itself.

Thus he was as unimpressed by the Marxist claim that the state was 'essentially' capitalist as he was by Hayek's claim that the socialist state was 'essentially' totalitarian. His answer to both was that the state was 'an instrument, and nothing more', and it was a piece of 'bluff', whether from Hegel or Hayek, Marx or Freud, to present it as anything else:

> Fools will use it, when they can, for foolish ends, criminals for criminal ends. Sensible and decent men will use it for ends which are sensible and decent. We, in England, have repeatedly re-made the State, and are re-making it now, and shall re-make it again. Why, in heaven's name, should we be afraid of it?[19]

He was to use the experience of the 1945 Labour Government as the definitive answer delivered by 'events' to such arguments, the confirmation of the mere instrumentality of the state. It had, contrary to Hayek's warnings, served as an agency for the extension of freedom not as a road to serfdom. It had also, contrary to the assertions of Marxist intellectuals, proved eminently usable for socialist purposes. The general lesson from this period was that 'the public cannot be prevented by capitalist or other machinations from obtaining what it wants, provided that it genuinely wants it'.[20]

As ever for Tawney, the real task for socialists lay not in getting what they wanted but in wanting and willing enough what they could get. It was because this was the task that it was crucially important to develop that 'strong root of independent conviction' without which it could not be accomplished and sustained. Of course, this definition of the socialist project has been regarded by many other socialists (and many non-socialists) as exhibiting a remarkable naiveté, and as an absurd misreading of the actual situation in which socialists found themselves. Where was the historical analysis showing a future immanent in the present? Where was the economic analysis revealing the role of a changing technology and the process of exploitation? Where was the sociological analysis to demonstrate the centrality of class struggle? Where was the political analysis to illuminate the relationship between the state and the mode of production? Where was the cultural analysis to document the ideological dominance of ruling ideas and institutions? How could all this be set aside in favour of a simple (and simplistic) invocation to individuals to 'choose equality'?

In fact, Tawney was not innocent of such questions, even if he was not much interested in them. Some matters, such as the role of technology, he accepted as given. Of the relationship between economy and cultural life, he thought 'next to nothing'[21] was really known. The class structure in England he presented as mainly but not wholly the reflection of the economic structure, with the working class only a class 'when regarded from a limited economic angle', but with consequences for social conflict 'surprisingly similar to those foretold by the genius of Marx'.[22] What he did not believe or accept was that there were forces at work which were the real historical actors. The achievement of a kind of socialism worthy of the name depended 'not on the impersonal forces beloved of doctrinaires, but on human minds and wills', above all on 'the good sense, pertinacity, nerve and resolution of the loveable, pig-headed, exasperating Dubb'.[23] Tawney pinned his hopes on Henry, if only because he was the only credible candidate, but without offering any assurances about his historical victory:

> Since I am not a fatalist, and regard confident predictions from past history as mostly sciolism, I have not yet despaired of Henry. I consider it not impossible that he may one day wake up, make an angry noise like a man, instead of bleating like a sheep; and in England, at any rate, in spite of scales weighted against him, use such rights as he possesses, which he is more sensible than some of his intellectual pastors in thinking worth having, to win economic freedom.

Tawney acknowledged that 'a creed so obviously devoid of scientific foundations' would be regarded in some quarters with contempt, but it was his creed nevertheless.

Thus socialism (certainly a socialism 'worthy of the name' as Tawney was sensibly inclined to add) was made to depend upon Henry Dubb waking up, and staying awake. But why should he wake up? In some ways Tawney's metaphor here is quite inapt, even in his own terms, since he clearly did not believe that a historical alarm clock was set to go off, nor that a politics of Waiting for Henry was all that was required of socialists. Tawney rejected such notions as firmly as he rejected other notions that socialism could be achieved on behalf of Henry without waking him up. To exhaust an ailing metaphor, it was clearly Tawney's view that socialists should hammer away relentlessly at Henry's door, in an effort to arouse his mind and stimulate his will. There is a conception of the appropriate role for the socialist intellectual involved here, as the carrier of convictions, but, characteristically, Tawney is quite uninterested in theorising the conception. However, what he is interested in doing is to show something of what it involved in practice.

R. H. Tawney

If his time horizon was long, stretching out into an uncertain and indefinite future, he nevertheless had a coherent view of the process whereby the cultivation of minds and wills could be actively advanced. The role of education has already been noticed, along with the effect of welfare services in promoting a more vigorous population. Moreover, just as Tawney emphasised the psychological tonic produced by increased welfare, he also suggested that the psychological effect produced by victories scored against privilege and inequality was even more significant than their economic effect in strengthening the conviction in ordinary people that change was possible: 'Having seen inequalities, long declared unalterable, yield to social intervention, they will be less indulgent in the future to those which remain, and less easily duped, it may reasonably be hoped, by the technique which defends them'.[24] It is here that Tawney's own project comes most clearly into view. If the 'technique' which defended inequality, in conditions of political democracy, was to convince people that inequality was both necessary and beneficial, then what was required was a rival technique to convince them that it was neither of these things. This is what Tawney set out to provide. The question confronting the existing social order was: 'Given five fat sheep and ninety-five thin, how induce the ninety-five to resign to the five the richest pasture and shadiest corners?'[25] The form of the answer was ideological (not Tawney's term of course), and what was therefore needed was a counter-offensive conducted on this same decisive terrain.

Here, then, is the key to much of Tawney's most important work. It helps to explain its form as well as its substance, its characteristic strengths and its no less characteristic weaknesses. It explains why his argument was constructed not as an exercise in private socialist analysis but as an exercise in public socialist persuasion; and why it was less concerned to advance the credentials of an *a priori* moralism than to destroy the moral, social, economic and historical credentials of the *status quo*. The socialist project required a sustained and persuasive crusade of ideological demystification to deprive capitalism of the supports it had erected for itself in a democratic environment where it could not rely upon political coercion, and to equip people with the confidence and conviction to choose an alternative method of organising their economic system. This was the project which Tawney made his own, as he addressed himself to the task of shattering 'the halo of mystery which at present surrounds capitalism'.[26]

Writing about the Hammonds, Tawney identified their 'power of shooting a philosophy dead in a phrase'.[27] Yet the description is even more appropriate when applied to Tawney's own work. Intention and achievement, style and substance, all point towards this verdict. On every side the ideological underpinnings of capitalism are kicked away, with elegant irony and telling example. Homely analogies are deployed to press the argument home. The historical status of capitalism is revealed as that of an interloper. Its economic philosophy is shown to be a rupture from a traditional social ethics. The modern structure of private property is deemed indefensible in terms of the historical arguments about the nature of property ownership. On this latter point, there is a nice example of Tawney's argumentative method, not least in its use of history, when he notes that the defence of private property advanced by Lord Hugh Cecil (in his exposition of *Conservatism*) was 'of a kind to make his ancestors turn in their graves' since:

> Of the two members of the family who achieved most distinction before the nineteenth century, the elder advised the Crown to prevent landlords evicting tenants, and actually proposed to fix a pecuniary maximum to the property which different classes might possess; the younger attacked enclosing in Parliament, and carried legislation compelling landlords to build cottages, to let them with small holdings, and to plough up pasture.[28]

117

Further, capitalism is depicted by Tawney as no longer an engine of economic progress or productive efficiency. Instead, it is identified, along with the inadequate social philosophy which underpins it, as the source of social discontent and malaise. It can provide no principle of legitimacy or authority in social and economic relationship, and therefore exhibits an endemic tendency towards social disintegration and economic disorder. On every front, then, Tawney set himself the task of unpicking the web of ideological camouflage woven around the existing order, the removal of which would strengthen the minds and wills of those whose convictions were the only means whereby a new social and economic order could be achieved.

It is because this was Tawney's purpose that his work, certainly as a prescriptive social theorist, assumed the character it did. Its form was determined by the definition of the political project of which it was the expression. If it seemed less concerned to explore than to persuade, or inclined to set up its targets in such a way that the task of knocking them down became easier than it should have been, or to evade the questions posed by an intelligent defence of capitalism, or to present socialism as a project with many of the practical difficulties left out, or to declare as truths what were really hypotheses, or to be stronger on conviction than on substance – and these *were* characteristics of Tawney's writings, at least to some extent – then this is the explanation. While these characteristics should be identified, what would be inappropriate would be to evaluate Tawney's work as a different *kind* of enterprise from the one it actually was. If its purpose was to nourish conviction, so that more people might want to 'choose equality', then the considerable influence on minds and wills that it has exerted during this century might perhaps be regarded as its vindication. That was certainly the intention behind its construction.

There is a further aspect of Tawney's socialism of 'conviction' that should be noticed. This concerns the important role he assigned to political leadership. It was the task of socialists, and of a socialist party, to win the hearts and minds without which socialism was impossible. In order to make socialism it was necessary to make socialists, not merely to win votes. Voters deserted the cause when the going got rough (as it definitely would), but socialists did not. Thus political leadership had a vital role in developing a 'temper' in its supporters, for quality of support was even more important than quantity, which was indispensable for the durable political success of socialism. Labour would never be successful until it was backed by 'not merely a majority of votes, but a temper in the country which will see the job through'. Tawney believed that Labour's 'most serious weakness' was to be found in 'its attitude to the popular forces which should be its strength'. It should tell them frankly what had to be done, not bribe their support. It should warn them of the sabotage that would be directed against a Labour government which meant business, and how only a resolute demonstration of popular opinion would carry the day. Above all, it should regard democracy as 'a force to be released', the mobilisation of popular energy and will:

> The Labour Party, in particular, should think of it, not merely in terms of ballot-boxes and majorities, but as a vast reservoir of latent energies – a body of men and women who, when inert, are a clog, but may become, once stirred into action, a dynamic of incalculable power. Its function is not merely to win votes; it is to wake the sleeping demon. It is to arouse democracy to a sense both of the possibilities within its reach and of the dangers which menace it; to put it on its mettle; to make it militant and formidable.[29]

Here the theme is still the waking of Henry, as the socialist *sine qua non,* but now the emphasis is on the arousal role of a socialist political party. Tawney combines his call for a socialist political leadership to practice a politics of maximum audacity when in office with an insistence that out of office it should concentrate its efforts on so cultivating its support that it became 'the spearhead of a strong body of conviction'.[30] There is even a whiff of Leninism, a version of 'consciousness from without', in this account of how the masses who are typically 'inert' and 'a clog' have to be energised by a 'New Model'[31] army of dedicated socialists. There is, however, an even more pungent repudiation of Leninism in Tawney's assertion that socialism depends fundamentally not upon the vigour of a vanguard but upon the convictions of a people, and that it also depends not upon the correct application of a science of history but upon the making of correct moral choices. Of course, in classical Marxist terms, Tawney's position represents the worst kind of idealism and moralism, deserving theoretical pity and political contempt. Yet what deserves notice here is that Tawney's idealism is not merely stated in general terms but converted into an active political strategy, both for himself and others. Ideas had to be disseminated, convictions nourished, and wills roused. If he believed the battle of ideas was decisive, he also had a plan of campaign appropriate to the terrain.

It is clear, then, that Tawney made the role of 'opinion' central to his discussion of contemporary society and of the prospects for socialism. Interests were important, but they were not enough. If capitalism was to be replaced by socialism (it could, of course, be replaced by something else), this required that people (not defined simply as a class) should, in some significant sense, choose this historical option (certainly if it was to be democratic socialism, the only kind worth having). Yet Tawney was also an economic historian, who could be expected to give some attention to the interplay of opinion and interest, the moral and the material, in his discussion of the past. What was the connection between Tawney's history and his socialism? Was he an idealist historian as well as an idealist socialist? How did he present the relationship between opinion and interest in the past? Did he advance a general view of history to sustain his particular standpoint on the present? Without attempting either an over-view or evaluation of Tawney's historical work,[32] it is clearly necessary to say something about such questions in so far as they bear directly on the rest of his thought.

It is certainly the case, and of crucial significance, that Tawney's analysis of contemporary society was that of a historian who was also a moralist. It is also the case that, as a historian, he gave particular attention to the role of ideas, opinions and values. This was conspicuously so in his earlier work, and most notably of all in his edition of Wilson's *Discourse Upon Usury* and in *Religion and the Rise of Capitalism,* but even his final book was prefaced by a reminder that the solid stuff of commercial and financial policy in the seventeenth century with which it dealt had to be set within a framework of which 'not least important' was the place of 'political assumptions, aspirations and beliefs'.[33] He frequently suggested that the most fundamental level at which the historical record should be read was that of ideas and values. Hence he could declare that:

> The difference between the England of Shakespeare, still visited by
> the ghosts of the Middle Ages, and the England which emerged in
> 1700 from the fierce polemics of the last two generations, was a
> difference of social and political theory even more than of constitu-
> tional and political arrangements. Not only the facts, but the minds
> which appraised them, were profoundly modified.[34]

Whether examining the upheavals caused by agrarian change in the sixteenth century, or the development of capitalism over a longer period, Tawney always wanted to locate the real issues at stake less in the empirical arena of 'facts' and more in the moral arena of 'minds'. In this sense, he clearly did believe that history was the history of ideas.

However, the belief that ideas mattered, even supremely so, and that the historical process should be regarded as a struggle of ideas and values, was not by itself a claim that ideas shaped the historical process in any independently significant way. It was quite possible to believe that ideas and values were important, and to illuminate their historical fortunes (with at least one eye on the present), without also believing that their historical status was that of cause rather than of consequence. At times Tawney does seem to want to make them key historical actors in their own right. Thus he reminds those who 'regard the history of opinion as an unprofitable dilettantism' that ideas can be 'a high explosive',[35] as evidenced by the history of capitalism no less than the history of socialism. He presents important historical moments in terms of the movement in thought of which they were the product, so that, as in 1918, 'not merely the facts, but the minds which appraise them, have been profoundly modified'.[36] Even when he came to revise his judgement on this particular period, his revision drew upon the same kind of evidence. War collectivism had not proved durable because it had been 'doctrineless', in the sense that it had 'not been accompanied by any intellectual conversion on the subject of the proper relations between the State and economic life'.[37] Similarly, when he discussed the nature of the world which was emerging after 1945, he found the real motor of change – away from pre-war capitalism, and towards collectivism – in the 'reversal of attitudes' which had taken place, producing a new 'set of British life' which was the active, historical force behind the process of change.[38]

Yet, at other times, Tawney seems to want to draw attention to the limitations of a historical analysis which, in its preoccupation with the movement of ideas, paid inadequate attention to the material forces at work. It was the fate of the classical liberal theory of private property, as it was of other political theories, to be refuted 'not by the doctrines of rival philosophers, but by the prosaic course of economic development'.[39] The study of ideas could not be separated from a study of the material environment in which they were framed, and 'doctrines with sufficient iron in them to survive are more often the children of the market-place than of the study'.[40] General statements of this kind drew support from Tawney's treatment of particular topics. Even when his main purpose seemed to be to emphasise the struggle of ideas and values involved in the events under discussion, this did not prevent his conclusions from underlining the extent to which the fate of ideas was tied to the fate of the material forces and social classes which carried them. This was the verdict on the struggle over enclosures. It was why Richard Baxter's restatement of a Christian code of economic conduct fell on stony ground. It was why the argument about usury was lost. Tawney's admiration for the struggles of moral resistance involved in these episodes, and his attempt to retrieve their arguments for his own generation, could not conceal the fact that these were struggles which had been lost. They were lost because new economic forces and social classes had been energetically remaking the world, including the world of ideas, in their own image.

When Tawney turned his attention to contemporary issues, especially when his purpose was to analyse rather than to exhort, he displayed a similar sensitivity to the importance of material factors. Two examples make the point. In the briefing he prepared on the nature of the American labour movement, he emphasised the extent to which its divisions were the product of 'impersonal' factors, notably the particular character of American economic development.[41] Then there was his account of China, in which – his admiration for the spiritual quality of Chinese civilisation notwithstanding – he emphasised that the country's ability to become a stable political unit depended upon its economic foundations: 'Political organisation rests on economic foundations; when the latter crumble, it crumbles with them'. He drew particular and prescient attention to the fundamental fact that the 'so-called Communist question is still very largely a land question', despite the 'doctrinal edge' given to economic discontent. It had little connection with the theoretical tradition of Western communism. Its future, like the future of China itself, would be determined by the land question and the peasantry.[42]

On one side, then, Tawney can be found insisting on the importance of ideas in history and warning against their neglect; while, on another side, he can be found arguing and demonstrating that ideas do not live in a material vacuum and that it is to the material world that the historian must look for the driving forces behind historical development. There might seem to be paradox, even contradiction, here. Was Tawney arguing that the world of mind was fundamental, or the world of matter? Or was he, perhaps, confused or inconsistent on the point? How could someone come to be regarded, *qua* social theorist, as representing a position distinguished by its emphasis on the pivotal significance of ideas and values, while also coming to be regarded, *qua* historian, as representing (and inspiring) a tradition of historical inquiry distinguished by its emphasis on the crucial importance of economic forces and social classes in historical development?

There are a number of answers to such questions. There is, first, the fact that Tawney was both a moralist and a historian. He believed, as the former, that values were what mattered supremely and should not be regarded as a function of something else. That was itself a moral position, uncompromisingly held, the rock from which he surveyed doctrines and institutions, the past and the present. He could also believe, as a historian, that the genesis and fate of ideas and values was profoundly influenced by the economic and social basis of a society. In a basic sense, these were different *kinds* of belief and should not be confused.

This does not mean, of course, that questions should not be asked about the viability of a politics which was required to accommodate both these beliefs. There is, secondly, the evidence of some shift of emphasis in Tawney's historical work, described by Winter in terms of a distinction between 'the moralist and the structuralist phases'[43] of his history, in response to a changing contemporary situation and the questions suggested by it. This distinction, although it should not be drawn too tightly, provides a useful corrective to the view of Tawney's thought as essentially fixed and immobile. In Edwardian England, and through into the 1920s, a concern with the social question led naturally to an exploration of the moral traditions of the past and an attempt to retrieve what was valuable in them for the contemporary world. That, at least in part, was Tawney's purpose in the period from *The Agrarian Problem in the Sixteenth Century* (1912) to *Religion and the Rise of Capitalism* (1926). However, the different world of the 1930s, a world of political turmoil and economic dislocation, suggested other questions, especially concerning the relationship between political change and economic and social development. Under their influence, Tawney's concern shifted from an exploration of the moral dimension of economic issues of the past to an identification of the structural economic and social factors influencing political change. This emphasis, reflected in his studies of 'The Rise of the Gentry' and 'Harrington's Interpretation of his Age', launched a whole tradition of historical inquiry and many celebrated controversies. His basic outlook remained remarkably unchanged, but this shift of emphasis meant that it could now be viewed from different angles.

There is also a third answer, which was Tawney's own, to the kind of questions asked above. It is not a theorised answer, in the form of a developed 'theory' of history (something for which Tawney had little taste and much suspicion), but it is a consistent approach to the historical process. It is best expressed in a phrase frequently employed by Tawney to characterise the movement of history, at particular periods but also generally. History, he liked to say, was a story of 'action and reaction', and it was in this spirit that he always approached it. In giving attention to structural factors, he did not cease to be a moralist. It was as an idealist that he provided the materials for a neo-determinism. History was dynamic, multi-faceted, interactive, and ambiguous. In particular, it was the interaction between the conditioning framework of the material world and the human response to the forces deriving from this framework which was the crucial historical arena. This was certainly the arena to which Tawney devoted his own consistent attention. His verdict on what he found there was that:

> The philosophy which sees the one constant dynamic in the pressure and pull of economic forces is a just nemesis on the facile sentimentalism of historical interpretations which idealise the flower to the neglect of roots and soil. But such forces are not automatic agents. They become a power, not directly, but at one remove, when passed through the transforming medium of human minds and wills, which are not passive, but impose, in reacting to them, a pattern of their own. . . It is with the human response, not the material challenge, that the last word lies.[44]

Thus human beings chose their own history, but from the range of choice which was materially available.

This general approach can be seen at work in Tawney's historical writing. Even in his most 'idealist' mood before 1914, the emphasis on the importance of ideas and values which distinguishes his discussion of *The Agrarian Problem in the Sixteenth Century* is combined with a sensitivity to the process whereby ideas can both be determining and determined: 'For though conceptions of social expediency are largely the product of economic conditions, they acquire a momentum which persists long after the circumstances which gave them birth have disappeared, and act as over-ruling forces to which, in the interval between one great change and another, events themselves tend to conform'.[45] If ideas are consequences, they also have consequences. Tawney's work is organised around this dual proposition. This is why it is misleading to invent a 'Weber-Tawney thesis' on the role of religious thought in the development of capitalism. If Tawney was characteristically fulsome in his tribute to the distinction of Weber's work on the importance of the Calvinist idea of the 'calling' in fostering the 'spirit' of capitalism, this could not disguise the fact that Tawney's own purpose was sharply different from Weber's, that he offered several lines of criticism of the latter's work, and that – most important of all – he regarded Weber's approach as ultimately unbalanced and one-sided in its emphasis on the role of ideas and beliefs: 'It is the temptation of one who expounds a new and fruitful idea to use it as a key to unlock all doors, and to explain by reference to a single principle phenomena which are, in reality, the result of several converging causes.'[46] As ever, it was a case of action and reaction: Puritanism helped to shape the economic order, but was itself shaped by that order. In *Religion and the Rise of Capitalism* the relationship Tawney described was 'permissive' (as Talcott Parsons well observed),[47] not determining.

In his 'moralist' period, then, Tawney the historian nevertheless kept moral ideas in their place. Likewise, in his 'structuralist' period, he resisted the lure of a neat determinism. He was, despite his historical reputation, a most unideological historian (as Christopher Hill puts it, he was no more a Tawneyite than Namier was a Namierite or Marx a Marxist).[48] He praised Weber, but then distanced himself from his intellectualism. He praised Marx more (and announced, in his inaugural lecture, that all serious history was 'inevitably post-Marxian'),[49] but then distanced the 'humanist' Marx – who was 'as saturated with ethics as a Hebrew

prophet'[50] – from both the historical method and political conclusions of those who claimed to be his disciples. A theory of historical development could not be converted into, or substituted for,
a statement of values. It did not reduce the status of ethics to
illuminate their economic origins. Further, it was illegitimate to
use Marx's method to press the historical record into a rigid
interpretative mould. Thus, while insisting on the centrality of
'capitalism' as a historical category, Tawney also insisted on the
need to be sensitive to its specificities and mutation. It was too
simplistic to describe the English revolution as 'bourgeois', not
least because the bourgeoisie was to be found on both sides.
Puritanism was a spur to capitalism, but it was not just that. The
achievements of liberalism were not simply the victory march of
the middle class. Tawney was impatient with historical writing
which seemed excessively doctrinal. He found Maurice Dobb's
history of capitalism flawed by its 'single-track presentation' of
the mode of production; and, reading Eric Hobsbawm's thesis
on the Fabians for a publisher, he found it 'slick, superficial and
pretentious' on the grounds that:

> Most historians are aware that they are not infallible, and reflect,
> in making their criticisms, that there are aspects of the subject
> which may have escaped them. Mr Hobsbawm seems not to be
> hampered by similar inhibitions. He has chosen, for some reason,
> to write in a somewhat patronising tone, as of one possessing *a
> priori* authoritative knowledge of the truth and correcting the errors
> of lesser mortals in the light of it.[51]

Tawney's history was interpretative, value-laden and present-
minded, but it was also eclectic in its approach and full of warnings
about the perils of monocausal explanations. The historical process had to be seen as a 'connected whole' of interacting causation,
which meant that 'the only adequate history is *l'histoire intégrale. . .*
which does justice at once to the economic foundations, the

political superstructure and the dynamic of ideas'.[52]

It is against this background that Tawney's mission to persuade people to choose equality should be seen. There was no historical process at work whereby virtuous ideas would triumph, but also no process whereby the class forces generated by economic development would issue in socialism. Socialism was an available material option, just as it was an available moral option, but it was only an option. Towards the end of his life he declared:

> I do not believe that any alchemy exists by which historical facts and tendencies can either be made a substitute for. . . judgements of value or directly converted into them. I do not share Marx's mid-Victorian conviction of the inevitability of progress; nor do I regard social development as an automatically ascending spiral with Socialism as its climax. On the contrary, I think that, in the absence of sustained and strenuous efforts, the way is as likely to lead down hill as up, and that Socialism, if achieved, will be the creation, not of any mystical historical necessities, but of the energy of human minds and wills.[53]

This was the verdict of both the historian and the moralist, which twentieth century experience had amply confirmed as far as any socialism worthy of the name was concerned. It made socialism a more difficult enterprise than many socialists suggested, depending for its achievement and durable success on its ability to persuade and convince. In this sense, socialism's project became Tawney's own, as he endeavoured to persuade his fellow citizens that, on both moral and practical grounds, it made sense to follow Dr Arnold's prescription to Choose Equality and Flee Greed.

6 *Tawney, Tawneyism and today*

'The world of today will not last'.

Does Tawney matter? Does he matter to us, now? In thinking about such questions, there is no shortage of voices ready to provide answers. When Mrs Thatcher became leader of the Conservative Party in the mid-1970s, the public advice to her from the right-wing journalist Peregrine Worsthorne was that she should read Tawney, on the grounds that she lacked an understanding of the fundamental beliefs of British socialists and that a reading of Tawney was the essential remedy for this deficiency. There is no reason to think that Mrs Thatcher took this advice and, in view of the lack of interest in Tawney on the Left at the time, she could well afford to ignore it.

The advice reflected a conventional judgement of Tawney as the patron saint of twentieth-century British socialism, with both left and right wings of that frequently warring tradition to be found worshipping at his shrine. Thus Hugh Gaitskell described him as '*the* democratic socialist *par excellence*'; while Michael Foot could write that 'those who might quarrel with Gaitskell about everything else would not dissent from that verdict'; and Tony Benn pronounced that there was 'none greater' than Tawney as an exponent of British socialism.[1] Those socialists who wanted to indict the British tradition for its theoretical and political infirmities could also regard Tawney as having a representative significance within this tradition, except that what he represented was a 'cliché-ridden high-mindedness'.[2] Yet these were really historical judgements, for in the period from the middle of the

1960s to the early 1980s Tawney's work had ceased to be an active force on the Left in Britain. His kind of moralism was out of tune with a conservative Labourism which eschewed general ideas and was devoid of any serious socialist purpose, but it was no less out of tune with the sub-Marxism, student social science and sectarian dialectics which seemed to provide the main resistance to the prevailing futility. The space available for a distinctive democratic socialism had contracted considerably, and Tawney's influence had contracted with it.

When that period ended, as it was bound to end, with Labour's political nemesis, Tawney could be lamented as a distant and forgotten voice. 'Many of those who go to the special conference. . . in which Labour is to settle the future shape of its own democracy will never have read him', wrote *The Guardian* at the end of 1980, with Labour's constitutional crisis in full swing, adding: 'Some will never have heard of him'.[3] What could scarcely have been anticipated was that Tawney, two decades after his death and two generations after his most influential work, was again to be at the centre of political argument in Britain. Yet this is precisely what happened in the 1980s, in a remarkable episode of historical and theoretical retrieval. Two events were decisive in bringing this about. The first was the formation of the Social Democratic Party in 1981, whose founders not only seceded from the Labour Party but claimed to have taken Tawney with them.[4] The claim, though no doubt genuinely made and perhaps helpful in easing a painful passage, was illegitimate. It was illegitimate not because Tawney would have dissented from their despair at the intolerant factionalism to which Labour had reduced itself, or the party's continued refusal to enfranchise its membership at the expense of the block vote of the trade unions (matters on which Tawney had robust views, robustly expressed), but for two reasons of more fundamental significance. First, Tawney was and remained a democratic socialist who held that the durable political task was to replace an immoral economic system with a moral one, whereas the Social Democratic task was evidently to effect an amicable accommodation with capitalism. Second, but no less fundamental, Tawney was and remained essentially a party man, who had decided early in life that 'the labour movement, behind all its froth and intolerance, really stands more than any other movement, for freedom today'[5] and never had occasion to revise this judgement. Even when he rebuked his party for its lack of socialist purpose, sectarian frolics and neglect of elementary political truths (and such rebukes would no doubt have been at least as sharp in the 1980s as they were in the 1930s), the voice was always that of the critical loyalist not that of the putative defector or potential opponent. Tawney, almost above all others, could not legitimately be converted from the role of lifelong loyalist to the posthumous role of intellectual emblem of a secession.

Yet the fact that the attempt was made served to bring Tawney back into the political ring. However, it was an indication of the seriousness of Labour's intellectual and political crisis at the time that few voices were raised in resistance or protest. The only response came from an old Left, including an old New Left, affronted by the political appropriation of part of its own tradition.[6] This was a historical skirmish, with little resonance for contemporary political argument. Then came a second development, which transformed Tawney from the status of a disputed historical antiquity to that of an active intellectual force on the Left. When the 1983 general election emphasised the extent of Labour's political collapse and disintegration, the need to undertake some fundamental political and intellectual reconstruction turned at least some minds on the Left towards Tawney again. Indeed, Tawney seemed to be the ubiquitous presence in the Labour leadership elections of 1983, prompting *The Guardian* to nominate Tawney – Tawney as the ideal double ticket. The new leadership of Kinnock-Hattersley amounted to much the same thing, for Tawney was to be the foundation stone of their attempted reconstruction of British socialism.[7] This raises some questions about his qualifications for this role. What, if anything, could a thinker whose ideas were formed in the first quarter of the twentieth century contribute to the reconstruction of democratic socialism in the last quarter of the century? Did he really offer anything more than a rhetorical repertoire of quotations, a substitute for new thought rather than a spur to it?

Certainly at first sight the answer to such questions looks distinctly unpromising. As a political thinker, Tawney's ideas have been judged to be 'derivative'; while, as an economic thinker, his writings have been regarded as 'stronger on conviction than on substance', offering no reliable guide to the economics of socialism.[8] There is no reason to dissent from either of these judgements, for Tawney was not (nor had pretensions to be) either an abstract political philosopher or an economic theorist. However, within his own field of economic history it is also reported that 'the Tawney tradition is in decline'; there are similar reports on the 'precarious position' of the 'Tawney heritage' in the field of social policy; and even in adult education a case has been made for the contemporary irrelevance of the 'Tawney legend'.[9] None of this suggests that Tawney is alive and well at the end of the twentieth century, let alone an indispensable contemporary. Moreover, in some hands, the charge against Tawney is not that of inadequacy or irrelevance, but of direct culpability for the economic malaise which has afflicted late twentieth century Britain. He has figured prominently in 'cultural' accounts of British economic decline, as in the rabid charge by G. R. Elton that *Religion and the Rise of Capitalism* ('one of the most harmful books written in the years between the wars') had exercised a pernicious influence: 'At least one generation, and that a crucial one, was given grounds for believing that everything that contributed to the greatness and success of their country derived from sinful selfishness and money-grubbing wickedness'.[10] In similar vein, Tawney's critique of the 'acquisitive' society is alleged to have 'helped to make a whole generation believe that the achievement of equality in the distribution of social goods was impossible within such a society',[11] and thus to have fostered a damaging misunderstanding in Britain of the nature of equality and welfare and of the conditions for their achievement. Again, if true, this would seem to make Tawney an unlikely candidate for a major role in a political environment dominated by the problems of an ailing economy. Should he not, perhaps, be seen as part of the problem rather than a reliable guide to a solution?

What is certainly true is that the critics of British socialism have correctly identified Tawney as their most significant target. His work represents an assault on the social and economic system of capitalism, and on the values underpinning that system, which is distinguished by its comprehensiveness and totality. A thinker who held that this system of values and practices was, in a fundamental sense, immoral, and who marshalled an impressive range of argument and evidence in support of this proposition, was clearly a non-negotiable opponent. The seamless quality of Tawney's work is important, the expression of its Christian roots and its consequent range of vision. As Raphael Samuel remarks, 'his Christianity gave him a sense of the totality of social relations – including their psychic roots – which a Marxist might well envy; and it saved him from triumphalism'.[12] When combined with his profound historical sense, this produced a dauntingly comprehensive indictment of the human inadequacy and historical contingency of the prevailing organisation of social and economic life.

What is also true is that Tawney's work, whether judged positively or perniciously, is appropriately located at the level of social values. The task he set himself, which he always regarded as the essential task, had been defined in his pre-1914 diary: it was the development of 'a general body of ideas', a consensual social philosophy, without which durable social reform by democratic means was unachievable. Those critics who identify him as the guilty man in the diffusion of a set of social values which they dislike thereby pay tribute, perhaps unwittingly, to the nature of his achievement in precisely the task to which he had addressed himself. Tawneyism, as a way of thinking about social values and their application, came to exercise an important influence on several fronts and over at least two generations in twentieth-century Britain. However, it is the conception of the task, rather than the celebration of its influence, which needs particular emphasis here, for it is this which illuminates the character of Tawney's project, and suggests something of its strengths and limitations from a contemporary vantage point.

Having decided that society needed a new social philosophy, Tawney set out to provide it with one. It also needed the confidence, energy and will to act upon it, and he endeavoured to supply this too. His terrain was human minds and wills, his method was persuasion, and his project was the creation of a culture of socialism. It was because this was the project that the role of a socialist politics was seen as important in advancing (or impeding) it. His persuasive intent not only led him to deal lightly with potentially difficult questions, and to suggest that the 'technique' of socialism presented no particular problems if approached in the right spirit, but also explains why he was anxious to demonstrate that socialism was not merely morally superior to capitalism but also instrumentally superior as an engine of economic efficiency and guarantor of social peace and contentment. His work, contrary to the impression given by some of his critics, was not dismissive of economic considerations but much concerned to argue that the moral inadequacy of capitalism carried with it damaging consquences for social and economic well-being. Similarly, he may have held, privately, that it was necessary to believe in God in order to believe in socialism, but this did not prevent him from constructing a public case for socialism in which God was conspicuous by his absence (except as an appendix for believers).

This brings the historical character of Tawney's project most clearly into view. Deliberately speaking in a local idiom, accessible and familiar, he can be seen as engaged in the enterprise of drawing upon the varied resources of a whole tradition and putting them to the service of a social philosophy capable of sustaining a public philosophy of socialism. He summoned up Arnold and Ruskin, and put Morris to school with Webb. He continued that nineteenth-century tradition of cultural criticism of industrialism but restated it in twentieth-century, socialist terms. Raymond Williams has described him as 'the last important voice in that tradition which has sought to humanise the modern system of society on its own terms'.[13] What he added to this tradition, besides a sharper political focus, was the armoury of the historian, which he deployed to such powerful effect, not least in putting the resources of a pre-capitalist society in the service of the task of constructing a post-capitalist society. He teased the English for their distinctive disabilities, but even this was a form of private, English intercourse. As an Anglican of the Left, he endeavoured to remind that religious tradition of its social gospel and of the need to make it an active force again in the conditions of the contemporary world. The moral tone of his socialism found an echo in many quarters, not least from that tradition of 'liberal socialism' (associated with such figures as Hobhouse and Hobson) with which Tawney established an important connection. His moralism meant that he represented 'a kind of extremism which the new Liberals found it easy to tolerate' and his books 'struck just the right notes among left-liberals'.[14]

On many sides, then, Tawney built from within, tapping the resources of a familiar culture to make the case for a common culture. In drawing upon a range of traditions, he also sought to extend them. In working within a range of institutions, he also sought to radicalise them. The Balliol-Toynbee Hall tradition was nudged towards the need for social reconstruction. It was as an old soldier that he stoked the fires of a radical patriotism. The Anglican socialist called the church to its social mission. A familiar moral vocabulary was deployed in the service of socialist values. The liberal tradition was confronted with the nature of power and property in the modern world and re-routed towards socialism. Englishmen were reminded of their history and urged to reclaim it. The assumption was that the materials existed from which socialist values and a socialist culture could be forged. The working class had its own materials to contribute to this process, not the least of which was a tradition of solidarity, but its task was to add these to the common stock not to wipe the board clean and remake it in its own image.

This directs attention to Tawney's audience, and to the style in which he addressed it. The precondition for social and economic reconstruction, as *The Acquisitive Society* explained, was the 'intellectual conversion' of 'Englishmen'.[15] References to what his pre-1914 diary had described as the 'average decent Englishman' are scattered throughout his work, and indicate his sense of an audience sharing a common moral sensibility who could be addressed in the terms of a common discourse. His was not a class appeal to a class audience, unless this is understood to mean an appeal to the reading classes. Henry Dubb occupies an important place in Tawney's argument, but clearly not in his audience. This conception of socialism as intellectual conversion may, of course, be a misconception of the scale of the task, the nature of the route and the character of the agency (as many socialists would insist) but accurately reflects Tawney's socialism of moral choice. The wider society was to be persuaded that socialism was the contemporary expression of its own best self (and self-interest). It could be addressed in its own language, with the argument patiently repeated until conversion was complete and conviction fired. Even Tawney's famous irony set the argument in a local idiom, a style of shared understandings and of exaggerated understatement. Faced with the conspicuous consumption of the rich, he reaches for a term of opprobrium and finds 'ungentlemanly'. Faced with an argument to demolish, he pronounces it 'not according to light'. Faced with infant mortality statistics for the working class, he makes a savagely ironic joke. People would know what he meant.

There is a further aspect of Tawney's project which needs particular emphasis. In making the case for socialist values to his own society, on that society's own terms, he held out a promise with a special resonance. It was the promise of social unity, one society, a common culture, real community. This is an indispensable element in Tawney's work, just as it constitutes an enduring theme in the traditions on which he drew. The nature of class in England, 'that accursed itch of class-difference, like the pea under the princess's mattress' as Orwell called it, had produced a singularly uncommon culture. Class differences, and the institutions which sustained them, put people out of reach of each other. Capitalism was the organisation of division in economic life. In hammering away at these themes, Tawney offered an argument for socialism which was not simply an argument for equality, liberty or social justice but fused these into a vision of an integrated society rooted in a set of shared values. Richard Titmuss (the post-war doyen of social policy and Tawney disciple) has argued that it was 'the demand for one society'[16] which was central to the historical movement towards welfare in England, and Tawney's work can be read in this light.

His message was that there could be no social unity without socialism. This was a message capable of making an appeal to people who wanted the former even if they were not naturally sympathetic to the latter. Tawney knew too much about human nature, and about history, to offer the promise of undiluted social harmony, but his argument did emphasise the prospect of turning a class society into a community of fraternal relationships and cooperative effort in a common purpose. The shared social values which were the condition for the achievement of socialism were also the guarantee of a solidaristic society under socialism. Everyone would be pulling in the same direction, or at least have no legitimate excuse for not so doing. In the trenches of the Somme, Sergeant Tawney had sacked his batman 'for slackness',[17] and his account of the socialist commonwealth suggested that 'slackness', or other deviations from the common good, would be equally inexcusable. However, they would also be unlikely. Once the dividends and royalties paid to the mineowners were eliminated, then 'it would be reasonable to ask that the miners should set a much needed example to the business community by refusing to extort better terms for themselves at the expense of the public'.[18] Once industry had been reorganised on the basis of professional freedom, then the result would be functional service to the community. This alluring prospect prompted Graham Wallas to suggest that the failure of such moral revolutions to occur voluntarily opened the way to those more inclined to engineer them mechanically: 'Tolstoy helped to produce Trotsky, and the Tolstoy-Morris side of Mr Tawney may encourage the Trotsky habit of mind in England'.[19] Even Tawney himself was prepared to recommend a dose of moral coercion when necessary. In a striking passage at the end of *The Acquisitive Society* he demanded that the church should vigorously police its members on the basis of a code of social ethics; and, a generation later, advised that a socialist government should not be deterred by the fact that industrial workers seemed reluctant to assume the responsibility of industrial freedom and should 'take the initiative, force the pace, and – I won't say compel – but persuade men to be free'.[20] This must not be misunderstood. Tawney's functional unity was emphatically not to be imposed. However, having made it central to his socialist prospectus, he was anxious that it should be delivered.

It is possible to detect a general note of anxiety in Tawney's voice during the last decade of his life. On the one hand, a 'modest pride' could be taken in the 'advances towards the conversion of a class-ridden society into a community in fact, as well as in name'[21] which was the appropriate verdict on the achievements of the 1940s. Much remained to be done, not least in attacking the massive inequalities of inheritance and education, but the gains were real and vindicated the political method by which they had been achieved. Further, it was possible to present 1945 (as Tawney did, deliberately assimilating Keynes and Beveridge) as the confluence and consummation of a whole progressive tradition and, in that sense, as the vindication of his own political project. On the other hand, though, it had become clear that what remained to be done was not simply more of the same. Partly, this was because the problems of 'machinery' had revealed themselves as more intractable in practice than arguments conducted at the level of principle had suggested. Thus, as far as nationalised industries were concerned, Tawney now conceded that 'the danger of top-heavy bureaucracy and remote control is, in my opinion, genuine' and 'effective supervision of these Leviathans by public and Parliament has hardly yet been established'.[22] This made it even more necessary to think imaginatively about varied and decentralised forms of social ownership.

However, the greater part of the problem was not one of machinery, but of spirit. The worry here was that little had been done to stimulate a change of psychology, status and motivation, in such a way that a socialist citizenship would be fostered and socialism become a vital force in everyday life. To a socialist who, like William Morris earlier, measured social change in terms of its effect on the quality of social life and the character of human relationships, the new world of the 1950s could seem very bleak indeed. Near the end of his life, in the 1890s, Morris had expressed 'doubts and puzzlement' about 'whether. . . the tremendous organisation of civilised commercial society is not playing the cat and mouse game with us socialists',[23] so that more comfort, betterment and quasi-socialist machinery became a barrier to the achievement of 'a real society of equals' rather than a route to it. However, if this did become a possibility it would only be because

> the working people have ceased to desire real socialism and are contented with some outside show of it joined to an increase in prosperity enough to satisfy the cravings of men who did not know what the pleasures of life might be if they treated their own capacities and the resources of nature reasonably with the intention and expectation of being happy.

Tawney had a close affinity with Morris, and also shared this sense of a possible false future as a dark historical option. If that future was 'merely a more widely disseminated cult of betting-coupons, comforts and careers, there might be some gain; but it would hardly be worth the century of sweat which, together with some tears, has been needed to produce it'.[24]

Tawney felt able to discount this as an immediate danger in the circumstances of the 1930s, but it had become a more pressing foreboding in the circumstances of the 1950s. Again, like Morris earlier (but without the latter's faith in the power of a 'scientific' socialism to make everything work out all right in the end), Tawney's own doubts and puzzlement led him to ask questions about whether the working class would, after all, settle for comfort instead of freedom, quantity rather than quality, more instead of different. There is a painful and poignant note in the question he tossed out to a Fabian audience in the mid-1950s: 'What do men really care about?'[25] He had always believed, and assured others, that the labour movement essentially represented a moral revolt against capitalism, a demand by human beings to be treated as ends and not as means. He had often declared that workers 'felt' the present industrial system to be a denial of freedom, and had argued that any proposed reform of that system needed to be sufficiently fundamental to incorporate an adequate conception of human nature and aspirations. Tawney's own question now suggested that he may have been wrong about much of this. Perhaps, in claiming to know what people felt and cared about, he had claimed too much. Certainly the evidence available now about the 'instrumental' attitude of workers makes it difficult to see them as engaged in a moral revolt. Perhaps the remark by Titmuss that 'the severest criticism of *Equality* as a social theory is that it would be easier to realise in practice if all men were Tawneys'[26] does suggest a kind of vulnerability, though this is not a suggestion Tawney would have liked or accepted.

However, what this leaves out of account is the role of a socialist politics. Reading the notes of his speeches in the 1950s, it is clear that Tawney had growing doubts on this score too. It was, of course, the period when social democracy was deliberately deradicalised, when the British Labour Party was once more tearing itself to pieces, and when a 'revisionism' (the monument to which remains Crosland's *The Future of Socialism,* published in 1956) was busily contracting socialist aspirations until they could be reconciled with what an expansive and domesticated capitalism could plausibly provide. Much of this clearly depressed Tawney, because of the dilution of socialist values involved, the sterile factionalism which was a substitute for intellectual renewal, and the failure of a socialist politics to be the carrier of a radical 'meaning system'[27] to the wider society in the way he had always recommended. Yet, in these circumstances, he felt more able to identify the absences than to supply the need. He returned constantly to the same themes: the neglect of 'quality' of life at the expense of quantity, the importance of an 'intensive' socialism and not merely of an extensive, and the need for socialists to appeal to human 'imagination' and not just to interest. When he expressed the fear that British socialism was becoming 'dehumanised',[28] it was on the basis of these kind of considerations.

Tawney had not given up, but he feared that others may have done. He continued to declare that the fundamental problem across 'wide tracts of thought and life' was 'the corrupting influence of a false standard of values',[29] but fewer people seemed to be listening. He believed that a shift in the balance of economic power had taken place (and judged that this was 'unlikely. . . to be reversed'),[30] but also believed that the essential socialist project remained unrealised. It needed to be restated and renewed, in contemporary terms, but this was now a task for others. Indeed, revision and renewal was, or should be, a permanent characteristic of socialism, for 'every generation of socialists requires to formulate its own version of the faith for itself' and he was, therefore, 'not at all perturbed. . . when. . . told that the socialism of my youth is out of date'.[31] However, this espousal of revision was also an acknowledgement of uncertainty, even perhaps of intellectual exhaustion. If Tawneyism had met this fate by mid century, could it plausibly be drawn upon as a source of socialist renewal at the end of the century?

This question prompts a number of further questions. Tawney had pulled together the resources of a range of local traditions and harnessed them to the cause of socialism, but perhaps these resources were ultimately inadequate. They had been able to deliver the Keynes-plus-Beveridge-state, topped up with a small dose of collectivism, but nothing beyond. That other local tradition, of which Morris was the most eloquent nineteenth-century voice and Tawney its most authentic echo in this century, still found itself as a minority tradition. Perhaps this was destined to be its historical role, a permanent opposition to the spirit of the age but without the resources to become a governing force, and even its oppositional force progressively weakened. Perhaps, too, in tying his kind of socialism to a particular strategy of intellectual conversion and Labour politics, Tawney's position represented a radical misreading of the nature of the task. Instead of the experience of 1945 standing as vindication of his position, it could also be regarded as evidence of its limitations, of the ease with which socialism could be contained, even in exceptional circumstances, rather than of its ability to make political advance. More generally, if the view of the state as a 'serviceable drudge' was an expression of the energy of spirit and conviction which Tawney thought essential for an effective democratic socialism, it was also perhaps the expression of a Balliol view of the political world which, when applied to the task of building socialism, carried with it an excessive complacency about British political institutions and their ability to be used by purposive Englishmen of good will, without radical reconstruction, for radical purposes.

Nor are these the only respects in which Tawney's position presents difficulties, certainly from a contemporary point of view. At a time when the socialist project in the West, and not least in Britain, is experiencing a major intellectual and political crisis, Tawney can seem a remote and unhelpful figure. Faced with the ideological offensive of the New Right on behalf of liberal capitalism, Tawney's jibes against Hayek scarcely constitute an effective response. There are two problems here. On the one hand, Tawney's argument does not engage with the argument for capitalism at its strongest points, where the emphasis is on its ability to provide a dynamic means of running a modern economy without political coercion. Tawney's own emphasis is on the moral deficiency and damaging social consequences of such an economic system, with the result that the arguments never really meet and Tawney becomes of limited assistance to contemporary socialists in an area where they are in evident need of all the intellectual help they can get. The claim is that capitalism at least works, and can be combined with political freedom, whereas socialism at the end of the twentieth century still cannot reliably make a similar claim.

In engaging with this claim, socialists who turn to Tawney encounter the second problem with his position. What he offers is an argument that *in principle* socialism is superior to capitalism and that, once the battle of principle is won, then secondary matters of technique and machinery will soon yield (subject always to the exigencies of human nature) to Fabian administrative drudgery and a spirit of experimentation. There will be unity and diversity, planning and decentralisation, mobility and solidarity, equality and difference, function and community, freedom and direction: everything is complementary in Tawney's socialist universe, once the moral contradictions of capitalism are removed. He was in many ways the least innocent of socialists (who knew that the 'police collectivisms' had little to do with his kind of democratic socialism, even though he seemed to accept their economic claims), but his early century assurances carry less conviction to a late century generation which has learned the need to marry arguments from political principle with reliable evidence from political practice. Tawney (in common with most other socialists, including Marx) did not offer a developed account of how a democratic socialist economy would plausibly work (either as a command economy or a quasi-market system) or of the stages whereby a functioning capitalist economy was to be converted into a functioning socialist economy. He offered assurances, and reassurances, and the occasional note for guidance, but nothing more. Yet this matter is now central to the contemporary democratic socialist task,[32] when capitalism has regained its ideological vigour, when socialist economies are widely identified with both economic inefficiency and political despotism, and when the social democratic settlement has collapsed along with the collapse of the post-war boom which sustained it.

Tawney also seems remote from the kinds of empirically-based analysis, both economic and sociological, which informs discussion and definition of the contemporary socialist project. His case for socialism did not depend upon a theory of economic development, but it was located entirely within the framework of a single national economy. This location has come to look wholly inadequate as that economy has been internationalised by global capitalism, a fact which at least has to be incorporated into socialist analysis and argument. Likewise, his case for socialism did not depend upon a theory of class formation, but it did assume the existence of a traditional proletariat as indispensable socialist agency, with a supplementary note about the critical role of the 'brain-worker'. Again, this is scarcely adequate for a modern socialism preoccupied with the analysis of the decomposition of a traditional class structure. Where, and who, is Henry Dubb now? As economic historian, Tawney was much interested in the implications of economic development and social change. As social philosopher, he preferred to present socialism in terms of a universally available moral choice. A modern socialism ought properly to be concerned with both.

Where, by the way, is the female Dubb in Tawney's universe? There are far too many 'men' in his socialist argument, certainly for contemporary socialist taste, and a conspicuous absence of women (except, when needed, as wives, mothers and children). No doubt he meant to write about human beings, but he actually wrote about men. No doubt he was entirely typical of his generation, but his generation is not ours. Nor is it simply a matter of style, revealing though that is. The fact is that the author of a socialist classic on equality did not mention inequality of gender, except – in passing – as something safely abolished in the past, and even when Richard Titmuss introduced a new edition of the book a generation later this was not an omission that he either noticed or remedied. The socialist focus was on class, and on the position of men in the wage system. This focus is too narrow for a contemporary socialism which, nourished by feminism, has learned to extend its range of vision from class to gender, from wage labour to domestic labour, and from class relationships to personal relationships. There is a larger reworking of the socialist project implicit in such extensions, against which Tawney can seem fixed in time and space.

There is a further, and final, problem which should be noticed, not unconnected with the foregoing. Tawney's argument carried with it a strong sense of a moral community, rooted in traditional values, expressed in its codes of personal morality, its religious institutions, and its structures of private life. His aim was to mobilise this moral community for socialism, which he presented as the authentic social expression of its private values. Further-more, he offered the prospect of a moral consensus as the basis for a socialist society of common ends. There are two problems here, of principle and of practice. Even in its own terms, it is difficult to envisage such a moral unity around common ends as either a practicable or a desirable proposition, at least in any effective sense or in combination (as Tawney also intended) with democratic pluralism and functional freedom. There has been occasion earlier to identify this as a source of unresolved tension in Tawney's thought. However, in contemporary terms, there is an additional difficulty with his socialist enterprise.

This turns on the erosion of the moral community, of beliefs and institutions, to which he directed his appeal. His assertion that belief in socialism depended upon belief in God may have been a private statement, which his socialist argument reflected (as in its take-it-or-leave-it approach to moral argument, and the fundamentalist character of its treatment of equality) but did not rely upon, yet it did indicate the extent to which he tied the fate of socialism to the vitality of established moral traditions. Now the problem is not merely that God has had a rough ride during this century, at least in the West, but that the basis for any kind of coherent moral community has become much more elusive. Secularism has advanced, but so too has religious pluralism, while moral diversity has increasingly flourished. Tawney's vision of the Church Militant mocks the reality of the Church Moribund, just as his vision of a vigorous popular culture mocks the contemporary cultural dross (a reminder that all of Tawney's institutions, from the WEA to the church, have experienced secular decline). Moreover, his argument took the form (as in *Religion and the Rise of Capitalism*) of an appeal from the established values of private life to a recognition of their implications for public life. Such an appeal could scarcely be made in that form today, when the structures and values of private life are themselves contested and when, on both left and right, the direction of influence is such that public life is invoked to press partisan definitions of the values and structures appropriate to private life.

In a number of respects, then, Tawney may now seem a rather distant figure. It is possible to see him as the product of a particular time and place, eclectic in approach and derivative in argument, engaged in a persuasive project now exhausted, bristling with limitations, and whose problems are not our problems. There is certainly enough truth in this picture to suggest that a simple (minded) appeal for a 'return to Tawney' as the solution to the difficulties experienced by socialists and socialism in the late twentieth century is unlikely to be adequate to the task. Like similar appeals for a return to the founding fathers, it may reveal more about the seriousness of present uncertainties than a confidence about how to navigate a course through them. It may even denote an intellectual evasion, rather than a serious process of theoretical reconstruction. Faced with an intractable present, and an unpromising future, the temptation is to take refuge in a secure past. Tawney, as the towering historical rock of the 1920s, provides an obvious landing place for British socialists in search of some hard ground in slippery times.

Yet Tawney is not merely a historical figure. If there is truth in the above picture, it is not the whole truth. Indeed, in important respects, Tawney remains an indispensable contemporary. The period since his death has not been kind to his ideas, but there are grounds for thinking that this period may now be over and that a new generation may find some interest and relevance in an old voice. In the post-war world, socialism was divided between an authoritarian communism and a social democracy which tied its fate to welfare capitalism. Tawney's kind of democratic socialism, which rejected the former because it was not democratic and the latter because it was not socialist, found its historical space severely contracted. Yet much has now changed. Marxism has escaped from its communist prison and is again available to fertilise socialism in the West. Social democracy has not proved to be a durable accommodation with a tamed and expansive capitalism, and has again either to prepare an advance or a retreat. In these circumstances the need on the Left to construct, and reconstruct, a philosophy and practice of democratic socialism has become both necessary and urgent. It is with this task that Tawney offers some valuable assistance.

The assistance will not be welcomed by those socialists who, often in the name of Marx, claim to have solved the riddle of history and regard a socialism of moral choice as a bourgeois distraction. Equally, it will not be welcomed by those who wish to believe that socialism can evade the need to replace private property as power with forms of accountable public property. Or those who are equivocal about democratic values, methods and institutions. Or those who find it impossible to combine an extremism about ends with an extreme good sense about means. Indeed, if one fact about Tawney is that he has been conscripted by both 'left' and 'right' within British socialism to sustain their positions, a second fact about Tawney is that if he is taken *as a whole* then he is capable, and capable still, of exerting a disturbing influence on both their positions.

He is also capable of saying some of the most important things that need to be said in constructing a case for democratic socialism, and saying them with a particular force and resonance. Values are at the core of the argument. Capitalism is an affront to the equal valuation of human beings and a denial of human freedom. It is a system of structured inequality and unfreedom, wrapped around with layers of ideological mystification. Yet it is also only a phase of human history, eccentric in its disavowal of a social ethics extending to economic life, and capable of being transcended by democratic energy and conviction. It is a structure of power, and the concentration of power represented by private property under capitalism deprives this form of property of its traditional justifications. Socialism is the attempt to extend democracy and freedom from the political arena to the social and economic, but this is most emphatically a matter of extension and not of substitution. Its method is democracy, and its structure is characterised by the diffusion of accountable power. Socialism offers the prospect of turning a divided society into a community, with a common culture as the basis for social cohesion and fellowship. However, there is nothing inevitable about socialism; and, even if there was, that would not make it morally desirable. It has its basis in moral choice, and its achievement and shape depend upon the energy of human minds and wills.

Such a bald recital does scant justice to the richness and texture of Tawney's argument, still less to the force of his personal example. As a young man in Edwardian England he had felt the social problem as a personal problem, and his obstinate insistence on the politics of private conduct is not the least significant of his contributions. As a moralist, he argued that social change was unachievable without moral change, but while others might draw comfortably conservative conclusions from this, Tawney's radical conclusion was that a combined enterprise of moral and social reconstruction was required. Similarly, if he argued the need to put material preoccupations in their proper place, it was as someone who understood the importance of the material world. The moralist was also the economic historian, and the continuous dialectic of ideas and interest, mind and matter, in his thought owes everything to this powerful duality. In significant respects he extended and nourished the socialist argument in England. Not only did he equip it with the armoury of the historian, but introduced and integrated important understandings of power, and of culture. His treatment of the relationship between equality and liberty has provided a reference point for all subsequent discussion. He also had important things to say about the procedural values of politics, including political argument ('brûler n'est pas répondre') and about the character of an effective socialist politics in England.

For all these reasons, Tawney's statement of democratic socialism is both impressive and durable. Confident of its own credentials, it could be non-Marxist without also being anti-Marxist. Unafraid of boundary markers, it followed arguments where they led and achieved a powerful synthesis. It indicted 'capitalism' and espoused 'socialism' without trading very much in these ideological labels, preferring instead to explore the contents of the boxes.[33] It eschewed a private language and cultivated a public audience. It could believe that its task stretched into a

long historical future, while also believing that it required strenuous activity in the present. It admitted its uncertainties, but
refused to make them an excuse for passivity or despair:

> There are moments when we all feel overwhelmed by the immensity
> of the enigmas now confronting us. But men acquire light, not by
> waiting for it to be given them, but by acting fearlessly on such
> feeble glimmers as they already possess. As long as they refuse to
> take the first steps up the hill, they have no right to complain that
> the summit is in cloud.[34]

It turned institutions into values, and converted the small change
of politics into the currency of large principles. It refused abstrac-
tions, and judged creeds and practices in terms of their practical
effect on the lives of individual human beings. If this test condemned capitalism, it also explains why Tawney's kind of democratic socialism was unattracted by other kinds on offer in the
twentieth century.

Finally, there may even be some particular reasons why, in
the late twentieth century and after a long interlude, Tawney
again emerges as a strikingly contemporary voice. One reason
goes right back to where his own argument started, in an analysis
of the consequences for social life of an acquisitive capitalism:

> As are the qualities which men covet, so are the defects which they
> must endure, for the defects are part of the qualities. If men are
> fascinated, as they may well be, by the brilliant prizes of plutocracy,
> they must bear the burden of its limitations. Poverty, economic
> oppression, and industrial strife are not superficial and transitory
> incidents of the present industrial order. They are an expression of
> its essential nature as fundamental as its mechanical perfection and
> imposing material prizes.[35]

If, for a long time, the promise of unlimited expansion served
to fix eyes (including socialist eyes) on the brilliant prizes, both

the collapse of that promise and the nature of the contemporary social malaise has created a new constituency for an argument about the burden of the limitations of existing arrangements. In such circumstances, a voice which directs attention to these consequences, which wants to talk about the quality of human life and the conditions for contentment and happiness, no longer seems old-fashioned. There is every reason why socialists should extend the vision of social cohesion, social values and a common culture in the face of a society (and planet) savaged by the rapacious and disintegrative forces of global capitalism. There is a widespread, and urgent, sense that it is time to return to fundamentals, in the way that Tawney did when, early in the century, he put the search for a 'right order of life' at the top of the political agenda.

This, in turn, suggests a further reason why he may have a contemporary significance. The fact that there is a new constituency for arguments of this kind is no guarantee that socialists will address it effectively. Indeed, many of them will be impeded by the heavy load of traditional ideological baggage they are carrying. Yet there is every reason to think that the future of socialism in the West turns on its ability to persuade democratic electorates, who have had occasion to learn something about the historical experience of both capitalism and socialism, that the kind of socialism being offered is morally attractive, practically viable, and relevant to their late century concerns. It is no longer enough to make a case *against* capitalism; it is necessary for socialists to make a case *for* socialism. This will not be easy for those who have expected history, economic development, a class or the electoral pendulum to do the job for them. They may have something to learn from a socialist who, again early in the century, decided that the socialist project depended above all on its ability to change ideas and values, to cultivate a 'general body of ideas' in society, and whose work was a sustained attempt to develop a public philosophy of socialism.

If this reading of Tawney is correct, then he is least useful when regarded as a detailed guide to the pressing problems of theory and practice faced by the contemporary Left. He is most useful when regarded as someone who provided some of the best reasons for making the effort to face them. Tawney, the man and the work, still enables people to say why they are socialists, and why they are socialists of a particular kind. Other people, of course, as Tawney once quoted Ruskin, are also still able to 'read my words, and say they are pretty, and go on in their way'.[36]

Notes

Preface

1 Margaret Cole, 'Saintly Socialist', *Books and Bookmen,* November 1974, p. 17.
2 *The Diary of Beatrice Webb, Vol. 4, 1924-1943,* ed. N. and J. Mackenzie, Virago, 1985, p. 360; entry for 8 December, 1935.
3 Tawney to Barbara Drake, 21 June, 1949 (Tawney Papers, 24/2).
4 Arnold Toynbee, *Acquaintances,* Oxford University Press, 1967, p. 88.
5 Michael Foot, *Loyalists and Loners,* Collins, 1986, p. 95.

1   The education of a socialist

1 T. S. Ashton, 'Richard Henry Tawney', *Proceedings of the British Academy,* XLVIII, 1962, p. 461.
2 The best account of this tradition remains M. Richter, *The Politics of Conscience: T. H. Green and His Age,* Weidenfeld and Nicolson, 1964.
3 Beveridge Papers, British Library of Political and Economic Science. Also Beveridge's obituary notice for Tawney in *Balliol College Record,* July 1962: 'Harry tried everything that I tried and more than I did. He pretended to be happy in a workmen's Club at Bethnal Green though I knew he couldn't be'.
4 Tawney Papers (hereafter **TP**), British Library of Political and Economic Science: Speech to Jubilee Weekend Conference of LSE Students' Union, February 1956 (Notes for Speeches on Various Occasions).
5 Ashton, *op. cit.,* p. 462.
6 **TP**: Presidential Address to LSE Students' Union, 1950s (Notes for Speeches on Various Occasions, 20/5).
7 A. Briggs and A. Macartney, *Toynbee Hall: The First Hundred Years,* Routledge and Kegan Paul, 1984, p. 71.
8 Letter, 2 March 1906 (Beveridge Papers).
9 R. H. Tawney, 'The *Daily News* Religious Census of London', *Toynbee Record,* March 1904, pp. 87-8.
10 Cited in Briggs and Macartney, *op. cit.,* p. 71.
11 Tawney to Beveridge, 20 September 1906 (Beveridge Papers).

12 **TP**: Presidential Address to LSE Students' Union, 1950s (Notes for Speeches on Various Occasions, 20/5).

13 See H. P. Smith, 'R. H. Tawney', *Rewley House Papers,* III, x, 1961-62; and L.R. West, 'The Tawney Legend Re-examined', *Studies in Adult Education,* IV, 2, 1972.

14 'The Workers' Educational Association and Adult Education', lecture given in May 1953 to mark WEA Fiftieth Anniversary; in *The Radical Tradition* (1964), ed. R. Hinden, Penguin, 1966, p. 86.

15 Oxford University Tutorial Classes Committee Minutes, 24 April 1909; Rewley House Collection, Oxford.

16 'The Study of Economic History', *Economica,* XIII, 1933; in *History and Society: Essays by R. H. Tawney,* ed. J. M. Winter, Routledge and Kegan Paul, 1978, p. 48.

17 E. S. Cartwright Papers, 17 February 1908; Rewley House Collection.

18 'Rochdale No. 1 Tutorial Class: Report, 1909-1910'; Rewley House Collection.

19 See the introductory memoir to R.H. Tawney (ed.), *Studies in Economic History: The Collected Papers of George Unwin,* Macmillan, 1927.

20 W. J. Ashley, *Economic Journal,* XXIII, 1913, pp. 85-9.

21 R. H. Tawney, *The Agrarian Problem in the Sixteenth Century,* Longmans, 1912, p. 347.

22 'The Assessment of Wages in England by the Justices of the Peace', (1913-14); in *R. H. Tawney: The American Labour Movement and Other Essays,* ed. J. M. Winter, Harvester, 1979, p. 130.

23 'Poverty as an Industrial Problem' (1913); in *The American Labour Movement and Other Essays,* p. 111.

24 'An Experiment in Democratic Education', *Political Quarterly,* May 1914; in *The Radical Tradition,* pp. 74-85. H. P. Smith described this article as 'the clearest statement I know of what he stood for in his early days as a tutorial class tutor' (*op. cit.,* p. 42).

25 Russell L. Jones, 'The Invasion of a University', *Highway,* August 1911, p. 173.

26 *R. H. Tawney's Commonplace Book,* ed. J. M. Winter and D. M. Joslin, Cambridge University Press, 1972, p. 29; and *passim.*

27 Diary of Beatrice Webb, January 21, 1939 (Passfield Papers).

28 J. M. Winter, *Socialism and the Challenge of War: Ideas and Politics in Britain 1912-18,* Routledge and Kegan Paul, 1974, pp. 153-4.

29 'The Attack', *Westminster Gazette,* August 1916; in *The Attack and Other*

Papers (1953), Spokesman, 1981, p. 16.

30 Tawney to Beveridge, 22 December 1915 (Beveridge Papers). Tawney also told Beveridge, from France, that 'on the whole I prefer to think of myself as fighting for this country than for England' *(ibid).*

31 'Some Reflections of a Soldier', *Nation,* October 1916; in *The Attack and Other Papers,* p. 22.

32 'The Conditions of Economic Liberty', in *Labour and Capital after the War,* ed. S. J. Chapman, Murray, 1918; in *The Radical Tradition,* p. 101.

33 *Democracy or Defeat,* WEA, 1917. Tawney's biographer, who is also a distinguished Sinologist, writes that: 'One may read Mao Tse-tung and Lin Piao, yet still feel that nowhere is there a better statement of what "people's war" means than in Tawney's *Democracy or Defeat'* (R. Terrill, *R. H. Tawney and His Times,* André Deutsch, 1974, p. 49).

34 'A National College of All Souls', *Times Educational Supplement,* 22 February, 1917; in *The Attack and Other Papers,* p. 34.

35 Tawney to A. L. Smith, 27 December 1917 (Balliol College Papers).

36 This comment by the historian W. H. B. Court makes the point well: 'It is difficult at this distance of time to make clear to those who never knew him or who never read his books when they were written the exceptional position held by Richard Henry Tawney in scholarship and politics in the twenties. . . He occupied as an historian a position half-way between politics and philosophy. This made him extremely interesting to young people trying to make up their own minds' *(Scarcity and Choice in History,* Edward Arnold, 1970, p. 17).

37 R. Barker, *Education and Politics 1900-1951,* Oxford, 1972, p.37.

38 *The Diary of Beatrice Webb: Volume Three 1905-1924,* ed. N. and J. MacKenzie, Virago, 1984; entry for 23 June, 1919. Observing the Coal Commission in session, Beatrice noted that Tawney 'raises the whole discussion to the highest planes of moral rectitude and sweet reasonableness' *(ibid.,* 12 March, 1919).

39 F.J. Fisher, 'Tawney's Century', in *Essays in the Economic and Social History of Tudor and Stuart England,* ed. F.J. Fisher, Cambridge, 1961, p. 1.

40 'The Study of Economic History', in *History and Society,* p. 63.

41 R. H. Tawney, *Business and Politics under James I: Lionel Cranfield as Merchant and Minister,* Cambridge, 1958, p. 275.

42 Ann Oakley, *Taking It Like a Woman,* Fontana, 1985, p. 19.

43 T. S. Ashton, *op. cit.,* p. 478.

2 Diagnosing the malady

1 On this history, see Anthony Wright, *Socialisms: Theories and Practices,* Oxford, 1986.

2 R. H. Tawney, *Equality* (1931), George Allen and Unwin, 1964, p. 26.

3 R. H. Tawney, *The Acquisitive Society* (1921), Fontana, 1961, p. 10.

4 'The impetus to reform or revolution springs in every age from the realisation of the contrast between the external order of society and the moral standards recognised as valid by the conscience or reason of the individual' (R. H. Tawney, *Religion and the Rise of Capitalism* (1926), Penguin, 1938, p. 118).

5 **TP**: 'The New Leviathan' (c. 1919-20, 20/10). This important manuscript is misfiled in the Tawney Papers. And *passim.*

6 S. Spender, *World Within World,* Hamish Hamilton, 1953, pp. 1-2.

7 *The Acquisitive Society,* pp. 9-10; and *passim.*

8 Coal Industry Commission, *Reports and Minutes of Evidence,* Cmd. 359/360, 1919, p. 575.

9 *Equality,* p. 73; and *passim.*

10 **TP**: 'Equality', Lecture to a WEA class, c. 1939 (19/6).

11 *Equality,* p. 108.

12 *Equality,* p. 102.

13 *The Acquisitive Society, p. 183.*

14 *Religion and the Rise of Capitalism,* pp. 219-20. Cf. Jeanette Tawney (ed.), *Chapters from Richard Baxter's Christian Directory,* G. Bell and Sons, 1925.

15 R. H. Tawney (ed.), Thomas Wilson, *A Discourse Upon Usury,* Bell, 1925, p. 15.

16 *Religion and the Rise of Capitalism,* pp. 18-19; and *passim.*

17 *Religion and the Rise of Capitalism,* Preface to 1937 edition, p. viii.

18 *The Acquisitive Society,* p. 121. This enabled Tawney to argue that 'changes which used to be urged for social or humanitarian reasons, and to be resisted on grounds of industrial efficiency, are now finding in considerations of industrial efficiency one of the main arguments to support them' ('Recent Thoughts on the Government of Industry', in P. Alden *et al., Labour and Industry: A Series of Lectures,* Manchester University Press, 1920, p. 195).

19 **TP**: Speech on socialism, 1930s (19/7).

20 'British Socialism Today', *Socialist Commentary,* June 1952; in *The Radical Tradition,* p. 178.

21 *Religion and the Rise of Capitalism,* p. 73

3 Prescribing the remedy

1 'Religion and Economics', *Times Literary Supplement*, 29 April 1926.

2 *Religion and the Rise of Capitalism*, p. 275.

3 Tawney to Mansbridge, 19 March 1909 (Rewley House Collection).

4 *Religion and the Rise of Capitalism*, p. 276.

5 **TP**: 'The New Leviathan'. This was 'where the mere economics of social reform – Fabianism etc – the whole "science of means" breaks down. They tidy the room, but they open no windows in the soul' (*Commonplace Book*, pp. 49-50, entry for 6 February, 1913).

6 'British Socialism Today', in *The Radical Tradition*, p. 178.

7 'The Choice Before the Labour Party', *Political Quarterly*, July 1932; in *The Attack and Other Papers*, p. 60. Socialism was 'obviously a word with more than one meaning' ('Social Democracy in Britain', in *The Christian Demand for Social Justice*, ed. W. Scarlett, New York, 1949; in *The Radical Tradition*, p. 146).

8 'Beatrice Webb', *Proceedings of the British Academy*, XXIX, 1943; in *The Attack and Other Papers*, p. 124.

9 *Equality*, p. 200.

10 'British Socialism Today', in *The Radical Tradition*, p. 176.

11 *The Acquisitive Society*, p. 15.

12 *Ibid.*, pp. 12-13.

13 *Ibid.*, p. 31.

14 *Ibid.*, p. 28.

15 *Ibid.*, p. 82.

16 *Ibid.*, p. 56.

17 *Ibid.*, p. 97.

18 *Ibid.*, p. 113.

19 *Equality*, p. 159.

20 **TP**: 'Equality', lecture to WEA class, c. 1939 (19/6).

21 'Christianity and the Social Revolution', *New Statesman*, 9 November 1935; in *The Attack and Other Papers*, p. 165.

22 *Equality*, p. 167.

23 *Commonplace Book*, p. 34; entry for 6 October, 1912. Elsewhere he wrote that: 'Freedom, to be complete, must carry with it not merely the absence of repression but also the opportunity of self-organisation' ('The Conditions of Economic Liberty', in *The Radical Tradition*, p. 107).

24 *Equality*, p. 227.

25 *Ibid.*, p. 228.

26 *Ibid.*, p. 232.

27 *Ibid.*, p. 235.

28 *The Acquisitive Society*, p. 149.

29 *Ibid.*, p. 129.

30 *Equality*, p. 175.

31 **TP**: Speech on guild socialism, early 1920s (19/7). Tawney defined his position further in a lecture under the auspices of the National Guilds League in December 1920, describing himself as a 'heretic' as far as Cole's pluralism was concerned (*Guildsman*, January 1921).

32 **TP**: 'The State and Minor Associations', MS notes, c. 1919-20 (20/10). In his *Commonplace Book* he had also noted that: 'It is evident that the fundamental questions of social policy in the future are going to turn very largely on the relation between societies and the state. No one now believes in pure individualism. Few are contented with pure collectivism. Hence the rise of various proposals for escaping the former without appealing to the latter. Syndicalism, gild socialism etc.' (p. 79; entry for 9 August, 1914).

33 *The Acquisitive Society*, pp. 124-5.

34 R. H. Tawney, *The Western Political Tradition*, Burge Memorial Lecture, SCM Press, 1949, p. 17.

35 **TP**: 'Equality', WEA lecture, late 1930s (19/6).

36 *Equality*, p. 29.

37 *Ibid.*, p. 49.

38 *Ibid.*, p. 136.

39 *Ibid.*, p. 74.

40 *Ibid.*, p. 144.

41 *Ibid.*, pp. 105-6.

42 *Ibid.*, p. 110.

43 *Ibid.*, p. 113.

44 *Ibid.*, p. 43.

45 F.A. Iremonger, *William Temple: His Life and Letters*, Oxford, 1948, p. 439.

46 *Equality*, p. 119.

47 'Social Democracy in Britain', in *The Radical Tradition*, p. 174.   He insisted that 'the greatest single obstacle to the efficiency of industry is precisely the industrial autocracy which is supposed today to be the condition of attaining it' ('The Conditions of Economic Liberty', in *The Radical Tradition*, p. 110).

48 *The Acquisitive Society*, p. 13.
49 *Religion and the Rise of Capitalism*, p. 225.
50 *Equality*, pp. 55-6.
51 *Ibid.*, p. 57.

4   Ends and means

1 'An Experiment in Democratic Education', in *The Radical Tradition*, p. 76.
2 'A Note on Christianity and the Social Order' (1937), in *The Attack and Other Papers*, p. 170.
3 'Social Democracy in Britain', in *The Radical Tradition*, pp. 145-6.
4 *Equality*, p. 39.
5 *The Agrarian Problem in the Sixteenth Century*, p. 409.
6 'We Mean Freedom', Fabian Lecture, 1944, published in C. Latham *et al.*, *What Labour Could Do*, Routledge, 1945; in *The Attack and Other Papers*, p. 87.
7 *Equality*, p. 85.
8 *Ibid*, p. 164.
9 'Christianity and the Social Revolution', in *The Attack and Other Papers*, p. 165.
10 'The Condition of China', Earl Grey Memorial Lecture, Armstrong College, Newcastle upon Tyne, March 1933; in *The American Labour Movement and Other Esssays*, p. 187.
11 R. H. Tawney, *Land and Labour in China*, George Allen and Unwin, 1932, p. 164.
12 *Ibid.*, p. 171.
13 *Ibid.*, p. 194.
14 'An Experiment in Democratic Education', in *The Radical Tradition*, p. 78.
15 'Some Reflections of a Soldier' (1916), in *The Attack and Other Papers*, p. 27; 'Why Britain Fights', *New York Times*, 21 July 1940, in *The Attack and Other Papers*, p. 74.
16 'The Conditions of Economic Liberty', in *The Radical Tradition*, p. 112.
17 *Ibid.*, p. 116.
18 *Commonplace Book*, p. 17; entry for June, 1912.
19 *Equality*, p. 27.
20 *The Agrarian Problem in the Sixteenth Century*, p. 409.
21 'British Socialism Today', in *The Radical Tradition*, p. 177.
22 *The Acquisitive Society*, p. 10.
23 'Keep the Workers' Children in their Place', *Daily News*, 14 February 1918; in *The Radical Tradition*, p. 52.

24 **TP**: Speech to William Temple Society, 1949 (19/6).

25 'A Note on Christianity and the Social Order', in *The Attack and Other Papers*, p. 170.

26 'China, 1930-31', *Manchester Guardian*, 18-23 May 1931; in *The Attack and Other Papers*, p. 48.

27 *The Nationalisation of the Coal Industry*, Labour Party, 1919; in *The Radical Tradition*, pp. 139-40.

28 'British Socialism Today', in *The Radical Tradition*, p. 184.

29 *Equality*, p. 119.

30 *Ibid.*, p. 230.

31 *Ibid.*, p. 145.

32 R. H. Tawney, *Some Thoughts on the Economics of Public Education*, Hobhouse Memorial Lecture, 1938, p. 9. Cf. R. Barker, *Education and Politics*, pp. 76-7.

33 *Manchester Guardian*, leader, 31 March 1945; quoted, and attributed to Tawney, by Barker, *op. cit.*, p. 80.

34 B. Simon, *Education and the Labour Movement 1870-1920*, Lawrence and Wishart, 1965, p. 362.

35 'We Mean Freedom', in *The Attack and Other Papers*, p. 99.

36 'Christianity and the Social Revolution', in *The Attack and Other Papers*, p. 163.

37 *Ibid.*, p. 165.

38 *Ibid.*, p. 164.

39 *Ibid.*, p. 163.

40 Diary of Beatrice Webb, 11 July, 1940 (Passfield Papers).

41 *Equality*, p. 221.

42 'Social Democracy in Britain', in *The Radical Tradition*, p. 165.

43 'The Choice Before the Labour Party', in *The Attack and Other Papers*, p. 56.

44 *Equality*, p. 203.

45 **TP**: Speech on Socialist Philosophy, 1930s (19/7). Unlike Orwell, though, Tawney's criticisms of left-wing intellectuals were discriminating. Orwell's biographer observes that Orwell would have gained much from a familiarity with Tawney's kind of democratic socialism (Bernard Crick, *George Orwell: A Life*, Secker and Warburg, 1980, pp. 204-5).

46 A. MacIntyre, 'The Socialism of R.H. Tawney' in *Against the Self-Images of the Age*, Duckworth, 1971, pp. 40-1.

47 P. Williams, *Hugh Gaitskell*, Oxford University Press, 1982, p. 373.

48 **TP**: 'Philosophy of Socialism', speech to London University Fabian Society, 1950 or 1951, (19/2).

49 'Social Democracy in Britain', in *The Radical Tradition,* p. 171.

5 Choosing equality

1 R. H. Tawney ed., Thomas Wilson, *A Discourse Upon Usury,* p. 104.
2 *The Acquisitive Society,* p. 10.
3 *Ibid.,* p. 66
4 *Equality,* pp. 159-60.
5 *Ibid.,* p. 120.
6 **TP**: 'Philosophy of Socialism', speech to London University Fabian Society, 1950/51 (19/2). Cf. 'British Socialism Today' in *The Radical Tradition,* p. 176: 'The socialist society. . . is not a herd of tame well-nourished animals, with wise keepers in command.'
7 **TP**: Toast, Fabian Dinner, May 1954 (19/3).
8 *Equality,* p. 142.
9 *Ibid.,* p. 120.
10 *Ibid.,* p. 219.
11 *The Acquisitive Society,* p. 15.
12 *Religion and the Rise of Capitalism,* pp. 211-12.
13 For an argument that Tawney's 'role of the intellectual as moralist' did 'lead to his having a considerable impact', see J. A. Hall, 'The Roles and Influence of Political Intellectuals: Tawney vs. Sidney Webb', *British Journal of Sociology,* 28, 3, September 1977.
14 *The Acquisitive Society,* p. 159.
15 *Equality,* pp. 40-1.
16 'British Socialism Today', in *The Radical Tradition,* p. 185.
17 *Equality,* p. 41.
18 *Equality,* p. 207; 'The Choice Before the Labour Party', in *The Attack and Other Papers,* p. 64.
19 'Social Democracy in Britain', in *The Radical Tradition,* p. 172. Tawney takes further issue with Hayek, and with all essentialist accounts of the 'instrument' of the state, in 'We Mean Freedom', *The Attack and Other Papers,* esp. pp. 93-100.
20 *Equality,* p. 223. Further, 'Parliament and the Civil Service will do the job for it; nor need it fear that the political machine will break in its hand' (p. 224).
21 *Social History and Literature,* lecture to National Book League, Cambridge University Press, 1950; in *The Radical Tradition,* p. 219.
22 *Equality,* pp. 63, 67, 118.

23 'Christianity and the Social Revolution', in *The Attack and Other Papers*, p. 166.

24 *Equality*, p. 150.

25 *Ibid.*, p. 150.

26 *Ibid.*, p. 205.

27 Tawney to Hammonds, 26 February 1917, quoted in P. Clarke, *Liberals and Social Democrats*, Cambridge, 1978, p. 188. Cf. 'J.L. Hammond', *Proceedings of the British Academy*, XLVI, 1960; in *History and Society*, pp. 229-54.

28 *The Acquisitive Society*, pp. 54-5.

29 *Equality*, pp. 202-10.

30 *Ibid.*, p. 203.

31 'The Choice Before the Labour Party', in *The Attack and Other Papers*, p. 62.

32 Tawney's historical work is reviewed in J. M. Winter's introduction ('Tawney the Historian') to *History and Society*, pp. 1-40.

33 *Business and Politics under James I: Lionel Cranfield as Merchant and Minister*, p. vii.

34 *The Acquisitive Society*, p. 17.

35 R. H. Tawney, 'Introduction' to M. Beer, *A History of British Socialism*, Vol. I, Bell, 1929, pp. xvi-xvii. Thus capitalism in Britain 'arose. . . in a country which was intellectually prepared to receive it. It developed, not by a fortuitous series of technical discoveries, but through the concentration of thought upon definite problems to the exclusion of others, and there is a sense in which Locke and Blackstone were as truly its pioneers as Arkwright and Crompton' (p. xvii).

36 'The Conditions of Economic Liberty', in *The Radical Tradition*, pp. 101-102.

37 'The Abolition of Economic Controls, 1918–21', *Economic History Review*, XIII, 1943; in *History and Society*, p. 142.

38 'Social Democracy in Britain', in *The Radical Tradition*, pp. 145, 161.

39 *The Acquisitive Society*, p. 70.

40 'Introduction' to J. P. Mayer, *Political Thought: The European Tradition*, Dent, 1939, p. vii.

41 'The American Labour Movement' (1942) in *The American Labour Movement and Other Essays*, p. 25.

42 'The Condition of China', in *The American Labour Movement and Other Essays*, p. 198; 'China, 1930-31', in *The Attack and Other Papers*, p. 49.

43 J. M. Winter, 'Introduction' to *History and Society*, p. 33.

44 *The Western Political Tradition*, p. 17.

45 *The Agrarian Problem in the Sixteenth Century*, p. 4.

46 'Max Weber and the Spirit of Capitalism', Foreword to Max Weber, *The*

Protestant Ethic and the Spirit of Capitalism (1930), in *History and Society,* p. 194. Tawney restated his reservations about Weber in his Preface to the 1937 edition of *Religion and the Rise of Capitalism,* pp. vii-xiii.

47 Talcott Parsons, 'In Memoriam: Richard Henry Tawney', *American Sociological Review,* 27, 1962, p. 889.

48 Christopher Hill, *The Collected Essays of Christopher Hill, Vol. 3: People and Ideas in 17th Century England,* Harvester, 1986, p. 24.

49 'The Study of Economic History', in *History and Society,* p. 51. However, there was also a pre-Marxian history. Hence Tawney's description of Marx as 'the last of the Schoolmen' (*Religion and the Rise of Capitalism,* p. 48), and his identification of 'the forgotten armoury of pre-Marxian Socialism' ('William Lovett' (1920), in *The Radical Tradition,* p. 24).

50 'Christianity and the Social Revolution', in *The Attack and Other Papers,* p. 160.

51 'A History of Capitalism', *Economic History Review* (1950), in *History and Society,* p. 209; **TP**: Report on Hobsbawm's 'Fabianism and the Fabians' (6/11). Tawney's own approach is reflected in remarks about his book on Lionel Cranfield made to Beveridge: Despite beginning with a 'prejudice' against 'a capitalist on the make', he 'ended with a respect for a man who, without being overscrupulous in business, was in courage and public spirit head and shoulders above the awful gang of courtly sharks and toadies with whom, as a minister of the crown, he was condemned to mix, and sacrificed his career for the service of the state' (Tawney to Beveridge, 27 January 1961; Beveridge Papers).

52 'The Study of Economic History', in *History and Society,* p. 64.

53 'British Socialism Today', in *The Radical Tradition,* p. 178.

6 Tawney, Tawneyism and today

1 H. Gaitskell, Tawney Memorial Service, 8 February 1962, in *The Radical Tradition* ('Postscript'), p. 221; M. Foot, *Loyalists and Loners,* Collins, 1986, p. 96; T. Benn, 'Foreword' to *The Attack and Other Papers,* 1981.

2 A. MacIntyre, *op. cit.,* p. 39.

3 'Tawney Across the Decades', *The Guardian,* 2 December, 1980.

4 Hence the formation of a 'Tawney Society' as the SDP counterpart to the Fabian Society. Shirley Williams gave Tawney a leading place among 'the great philosophic exponents of social democracy' (*Politics Is For People,* Penguin, 1981, p. 23). See also, Michael Young, 'Why the SDP are the Inheritors of Tawney's Libertarian Legacy', *The Guardian,* 10 May, 1982.

5 *Commonplace Book,* p. 47, entry for 2 December, 1912.
6 Thus Michael Foot (*op. cit.,* p. 92) was 'outraged' to hear that the Social
  Democrats intended to name a society after Tawney and 'took immediate
  steps to stamp on this preposterous insult to his memory'. These steps,
  it seemed, consisted of a letter to *The Times.* In two long articles in *The
  Guardian* (29 March and 5 April, 1982), Raphael Samuel sought to
  demonstrate that the SDP's appropriation of Tawney was to be seen as
  'an exercise in generating fictitious moral capital rather than the acknowledgement of a spiritual debt'.
7 Tawney figures prominently in Neil Kinnock, *The Future of Socialism,* Fabian
  Society, Tract 509, 1986; and in Roy Hattersley, *Choose Freedom: The Future
  for Democratic Socialism,* Michael Joseph, 1987.
8 W. H. Greenleaf, *The British Political Tradition Vol. 2: The Ideological Heritage,*
  Methuen, 1983, p. 440; D. Reisman, *State and Welfare: Tawney, Galbraith
  and Adam Smith,* Macmillan, 1982, p. 117.
9 J. M. Winter, *History and Society,* p. 34; A. H. Halsey, 'R. H. Tawney', in
  A. H. Halsey (ed.), *Traditions of Social Policy,* Blackwell, 1976, p. 254; L.
  West, 'The Tawney Legend Re-examined', *Studies in Adult Education,* 4,
  October 1972.
10 G. R. Elton, *Times Literary Supplement,* 11 February, 1977. Tawney's role
   is also identified in M. Wiener, *English Culture and the Decline of the Industrial
   Spirit 1850-1980,* Cambridge, 1981, pp. 115-116.
11 N. Johnson, *In Search of the Constitution: Reflections on State and Society in
   Britain,* Methuen, 1980, pp. 14-15.
12 R. Samuel, *op. cit.*
13 R. Williams, *Culture and Society 1780-1950,* Penguin, 1961, p. 223.
14 P. Clarke, *Liberals and Social Democrats,* p. 160; M. Freeden, *Liberalism Divided:
   A Study in British Political Thought 1914-1939,* Clarendon, Oxford, 1986, p.
   317.
15 *The Acquisitive Society,* p. 176.
16 R. Titmuss, *Commitment to Welfare,* George Allen and Unwin, 1968, p. 191.
17 'The Attack', in *The Attack and Other Papers,* p. 16.
18 *The Acquisitive Society,* p. 136.
19 *Nation,* 11 June 1921; quoted in P. Clarke, *op.cit.,* pp. 218-19.
20 'British Socialism Today', in *The Radical Tradition,* p. 185. Both individual
   and corporate selfishness could afflict workers no less than capitalists, and
   had to be overcome: 'Self-indulgence, irregular habits, scamped work,
   gambling and other futilities, the attempt to take from the common pool

without an equivalent contribution to it – such failings are not more edifying in a million wage-earners than when displayed by a handful of monopolists, speculators and urban landlords' ('A Note on Christianity and the Social Order', in *The Attack and Other Papers,* p. 190).

21 *Equality,* p. 222.

22 'British Socialism Today', in *The Radical Tradition,* pp. 182-3.

23 William Morris, *Communism* (1893), in A. L. Morton ed., *Political Writings of William Morris,* Lawrence and Wishart, 1979, p. 229.

24 'A Note on Christianity and the Social Order', in *The Attack and Other Papers,* p. 191.

25 **TP**: Toast, Fabian Dinner, May 1954 (19/3).

26 R. Titmuss, F. J. Fisher and J. R. Williams, *R. H. Tawney: A Portrait By Several Hands,* 1960 (privately published), p. 33.

27 Frank Parkin, *Class Inequality and Political Order,* Paladin, 1972. Parkin's phrase well expresses Tawney's conception of the role of a socialist politics, the retreat from which in the post-war period was to be seen, in historical terms, as 'a major transformation in the moral and political outlook of the socialist movement' (p. 127).

28 **TP**: Speech to London University Fabian Society, 1950/51 (19/2); Speech to Central London Fabian Society, 1950 (19/3).

29 'British Socialism Today', in *The Radical Tradition,* p. 188.

30 'The Workers' Educational Association and Adult Education' (1953); in *The Radical Tradition,* p. 92. Capitalism remained capitalism, but 'the identity of name masks a reluctant acquisition. . . of a slightly less unsocial nature' ('A History of Capitalism' (1950), in *History and Society,* p. 214).

31 **TP**: Speeches, 1950s, at LSE and St Pancras Labour Party (19/5).

32 On this, see A. Nove, *The Economics of Feasible Socialism,* Allen and Unwin, 1983; and G. Hodgson, *The Democratic Economy: A New Look at Planning, Markets and Power,* Penguin, 1984.

33 'If. . . a philosophy of Socialism involves the possession of a compact body of coherent doctrine. . . then candour compels me to confess that that convenient article has been omitted from my luggage' (**TP**: 'Philosophy of Socialism', Speech to London University Fabian Society, 1950/51, 19/2).

34 **TP**: Speech to William Temple Society, 1949, (19/6).

35 'The Conditions of Economic Liberty', in *The Radical Tradition,* p. 113.

36 'John Ruskin', *Observer,* 19 February 1919; in *The Radical Tradition,* p. 42.

Further Reading

Almost all of Tawney's most important work is available and accessible. In addition to his books, there are now several collections of his articles available. Although a number of interesting items remain outside these published collections, and his private papers (held in the British Library of Political and Economic Science, London School of Economics) account for a further twenty five boxes of material, all this really just fills out the picture of the man and his work which is abundantly visible from the readily accessible writings.

A full bibliography of Tawney's published writings is to be found in Ross Terrill's *R. H. Tawney and His Times.* This is also the only major study of Tawney's life and work and it manages, for reasons which this reader has never been quite able to work out, to be both generally excellent and ultimately unsatisfying.

Tawney's major writings are listed below (with year of original publication, as several editions of some are available), along with a small selection of secondary literature.

Books and articles by Tawney

The Agrarian Problem in the Sixteenth Century, Longmans, Green and Co., 1912.

The Establishment of Minimum Rates in the Chain-Making Industry under the Trade Boards Act of 1909, G. Bell and Sons, 1914.

The Establishment of Minimum Rates in the Tailoring Industry under the Trade Boards Act of 1909, G. Bell and Sons, 1915.

The Acquisitive Society, G. Bell and Sons, 1921.

(ed), Thomas Wilson, *A Discourse Upon Usury,* G. Bell and Sons, 1925.

The British Labour Movement, New Haven, Yale University Press, 1925.

Religion and the Rise of Capitalism, John Murray, 1926.

(ed), *Studies in Economic History: The Collected Papers of George Unwin,* Macmillan, 1927.

Equality, George Allen and Unwin, 1931 (4th ed., 1952, with new chapter).

Land and Labour in China, George Allen and Unwin, 1932.

The Attack and Other Papers, George Allen and Unwin, 1953.

Business and Politics under James I: Lionel Cranfield as Merchant and Minister, Cambridge University Press, 1958.

The Radical Tradition: Twelve Essays on Politics, Education and Literature, (ed. R. Hinden), George Allen and Unwin, 1964.

Commonplace Book (ed. J.M. Winter and D.M. Joslin), Cambridge University Press, 1972.

History and Society: Essays by R.H. Tawney, ed. J.M. Winter, Routledge and Kegan Paul, 1978.

The American Labour Movement and Other Essays, ed. J.M. Winter, Harvester, 1979.

Books and Articles on Tawney (or with material on Tawney)

T. S. Ashton, 'Richard Henry Tawney', *Proceedings of the British Academy,* XLVIII, 1962.

R. Barker, *Political Ideas in Modern Britain,* Methuen, 1978.

M. Freeden, *Liberalism Divided: A Study in British Political Thought,* Oxford University Press, 1986.

V. George and P. Wilding, *Ideology and Social Welfare,* Routledge and Kegan Paul, 1976.

W. H. Greenleaf, *The British Political Tradition, Vol 2, The Ideological Heritage,* Methuen, 1983.

J. A. Hall, 'The Roles and Influence of Political Intellectuals: Tawney vs. Sidney Webb', *British Journal of Sociology,* 28, 3 September 1977.

Further reading

A. H. Halsey, 'R. H. Tawney', in A. H. Halsey (ed.), *Traditions of Social Policy*, Blackwell, 1976.

A. H. Halsey and N. Dennis, *English Ethical Socialism*, Oxford University Press (forthcoming).

N. Haslewood, 'Tawney, the Labour Party and Educational Policy in the 1920s: A Reappraisal', in R. Lowe ed., *Labour and Education: Some Early Twentieth Century Studies*, History of Education Society, Occasional Publication No. 6, Leicester, 1981.

A. MacIntyre, 'The Socialism of R. H. Tawney', in *Against the Self-Images of the Age*, Duckworth, 1971.

D. Reisman, *State and Welfare: Tawney, Galbraith and Adam Smith*, Macmillan, 1982.

A. Ryan, 'R. H. Tawney: A Socialist Saint', *New Society*, 27 November, 1980.

R. Terrill, *R. H. Tawney and his Times: Socialism as Fellowship*, André Deutsch, 1974.

R. Titmuss, F. J. Fisher and J. R. Williams, *R. H. Tawney: A Portrait by Several Hands*, privately published, 1960.

L. R. West, 'The Tawney Legend Re-examined', *Studies in Adult Education*, IV, 2, 1972.

R. Williams, *Culture and Society, 1780-1950*, Penguin, 1961.

J. M. Winter, 'A Bibliography of the Published Writings of R. H. Tawney', *Economic History Review*, 25, February 1972.

J. M. Winter, 'R.H. Tawney, A Christian Socialist', *New Society*, 10 February, 1983.

J. M. Winter, *Socialism and the Challenge of War: Ideas and Politics in Britain, 1912-18*, Routledge and Kegan Paul, 1974.

A. W. Wright (ed.), *British Socialism: Socialist Thought from the 1880s to 1960s*, Longman, 1983.

A. W. Wright, 'Tawneyism Revisited: Equality, Welfare and Socialism', in B. Pimlott (ed.), *Fabian Essays in Socialist Thought*, Heinemann, 1984.

Index